Together Forever

God's Design for Marriage

Premarital Workbook for Engaged Couples

ED & ANGIE WRIGHT

Together Forever: God's Design for Marriage; Premarital Workbook
Copyright © 2003, 2015, 2017, 2022 by Ed Wright.

All rights reserved. No part of this publication may be reproduced, stored in a retrieval system, or transmitted in any form or by any means—electronic, mechanical, photocopy, recording, or any other—except for brief quotations in printed reviews, without the prior permission of the publisher.

Originally published as *Two Becoming One: Premarital Counseling Workbook*

Request for information or comments should be emailed to Angie@MarriagebyGod.com

Unless otherwise indicated, all Scripture quotations are from the HOLY BIBLE, NEW INTERNATIONAL VERSION®, copyright © 1973, 1978, 1984 by International Bible Society.

You can do more than plan your wedding—you can plan your marriage! Working through *Together Forever* is the best investment I know in your relationship and future happiness. You will explore and deal with issues ahead of your wedding day that might otherwise crop up as irritating problems after you are married. You will learn how to work through situations without being combative. You will appreciate your differences instead of allowing them to drive a wedge in your relationship. And you will learn how to show love to your mate in ways that he or she will truly appreciate.

Knowing the authors personally, I can assure you that the principles of this workbook are not only true to the Bible but also have passed through the sieve of practical experience in the lives of its authors, Ed and Angie Wright, who live what they write. This down-to-earth book will make a big difference in your lives from Day One throughout your marriage.

DARLENE SALA, *Author, Seminar Speaker*

Ask an engaged couple if they want a fulfilling marriage that lasts a lifetime, and they'll confidently say, "We do." Ask if they know how to make their desire a reality, and they may not be so sure. But they can be. *Together Forever* is the go-to guide that prepares and equips couples to enjoy the marriage they long for. As parents of newlyweds who benefited from Ed and Angie Wright's wisdom, we can't recommend their curriculum highly enough!

JP JONES, *Senior Pastor of Crossline Community Church, Founder of Truth that Changes Lives Radio Broadcast*

DONNA JONES, *National Speaker, Author, Bible Study Teacher*

It's all too easy for premarital mentors to sprinkle Scripture on secular philosophy or to present ideas they've never actually lived. But I've observed Ed and Angie Wright's relationship, and I'm impressed with their faithfulness to Scripture and the quality of their own marriage. They practice what they teach, and it has given them a robust relationship from which they help engaged couples prepare for a flourishing marriage. Every couple preparing for marriage needs premarital mentoring, and this workbook will help couples make sure that their marriage begins on a solid foundation. I highly recommend it.

DR. CLAY JONES, *Associate Professor of Christian Apologetics, Biola University; Chairman of the Board, Ratio Christi*

What others are saying about the premarital mentoring program
Together Forever | God's Design for Marriage

Ed and Angie's *passion* for premarital counseling was apparent the day I met them, over fifteen years ago, at Saddleback Church. God's anointing of their work has been even more apparent as their ministry, Marriage by God, has developed and exponentially grown over the years. Their ability to share their own life experiences in an honest, authentic, and often-humorous way provides all premarital couples with the true realities—and challenges—of married life. Written with solid Biblical principles, this workbook contains practical, easy-to-follow recommendations and insights on a comprehensive list of relevant topics. This workbook is a *must have* for all couples seeking a Christ-centered, fulfilling, and abundantly joyful marriage.

KATHY JO STONES, *Licensed Marriage and Family Therapist*

Pastors and churches who marry or minister to couples have a responsibility to do everything they can to ensure the long-term success, survival, and sanctity of the marriage covenant. That is the exact reason why I do not marry a couple unless they have been through *Together Forever* and why our church has installed it as a pillar of pastoral care along with *Putting the "Happily" Into Your Ever After* for already married couples. You simply cannot beat the combination of a trained Marriage By God mentor couple interactively processing the curriculum with a prospective or struggling couple. Every church that wants integrity in its couples or marriage ministry would serve its members and community well by installing Marriage By God.

KENNY LUCK, *Lead Pastor at Crossline Community Church, Award-winning Author, Founder of Every Man Ministries*

Many workbooks are written from a professorial kind of vantage as someone "blesses" the poor couple about to be married with advice. Not Ed and Angie Wright, who take you on their journey of the past fifteen years, sharing their foibles, mistakes, and rich nuggets of wisdom they have gleaned through personal experience. Their premarital mentoring workbook, *Together Forever*, is practical, Biblical, and loaded with insights that will be of tremendous help as you embark on the adventure of marriage. Having worked with couples for more than a half-century, I've read the good, bad, and indifferent books on "how to do a marriage." Theirs is in the "best" category. I recommend it without reservation. It can be a tremendous help in your relationship and future marriage.

DR. HAROLD J. SALA, *Founder of Guidelines International, Author*

Every couple that gets married should do premarital mentoring. Ed and Angie Wright have prepared outstanding premarital material. My wife, Dianne, and I went through this material thirteen years ago when we were married and were very blessed. Each couple will discuss all the important topics that couples should discuss, but sometimes avoid discussing before they get married. The topics include finances, sex, family of origin, making decisions, communication, resolving conflict, and others. The mentors guide the couple through a discussion of their differences on a topic and show how to reach Biblical agreement. This is the best I have seen and would recommend it to any couple either pre-engagement or before marriage.

TOM ATKINS, *Saddleback Church Pastor to Couples Small Groups*

As proclaimed in the name of their ministry, Marriage by God, Ed and Angie Wright's *Together Forever* premarital mentoring workbook and mentor's guide are essential for training engaged couples that seek to fulfill God's purpose in their marriage. Their mentor's guide reveals that not many should become teachers because God holds them to a higher standard. The Wrights represent the highest expression of God's intent for married couples, and I wholeheartedly endorse without reservation these two excellent books.

WILLIE NAULLS, *Pastor, Author*

Ed and Angie Wright have written a beautiful and biblical book on helping premarried couples understand the full beauty of God's plan for marriage. They masterfully weave personal stories and insights to illustrate the elements of a biblical marriage that are completely practical. I highly recommend this resource for those that are mentoring couples considering marriage.

CARL MOELLER, *CEO, Biblica - The International Bible Society*

We wish to dedicate this book to the Marriage by God mentor couples who have come beside us with a passion to help couples learn what it looks like to put Christ at the center of their marriage. You have humbly accepted God's assignment, and it has been exciting watching the Holy Spirit work in and through you as you pour blessings into the lives of couples preparing for marriage.

Table of Contents

INTRODUCTION — 9

SESSION One

CHAPTER 1	Two Becoming One	13
CHAPTER 2	Love Spoken Here	16
CHAPTER 3	The Freedom of Forgiveness	21

SESSION Two

CHAPTER 4	Putting Christ at the Center of Your Marriage	27
CHAPTER 5	Developing an Intentional Marriage	34
CHAPTER 6	Finding the Sweet Spot in Your Relationship	39

SESSION Three

CHAPTER 7	Personality Differences	45
CHAPTER 8	Differences between Men and Women	48
CHAPTER 9	Love Languages	53

SESSION Four

CHAPTER 10	Extended Family	59
CHAPTER 11	Communication	63
CHAPTER 12	Resolving Conflict	69

SESSION Five

CHAPTER 13	Emotional Intimacy	75
CHAPTER 14	Physical Intimacy	81
CHAPTER 15	Affair-Proofing Your Marriage	87

SESSION Six

CHAPTER 16	Finances	93
CHAPTER 17	Marriage Goals	105
CHAPTER 18	Keeping the Flame Going	111

APPENDICES

APPENDIX 1	What it Means to be a Godly Husband	119
APPENDIX 2	What it Means to be a Submissive Wife	121
APPENDIX 3	The Five Love Languages Test for Women	123
APPENDIX 4	The Five Love Languages Test for Men	126
APPENDIX 5	Love Languages Guide	129
APPENDIX 6	Rules for Discussion	130
APPENDIX 7	Ten Rules to Resolve Conflict	131
APPENDIX 8	Ten Ways to be a Fantastic Wife	132
APPENDIX 9	Ten Ways to be a Fantastic Husband	133

Introduction

IN 1999, AS OUR SONS WENT OFF TO COLLEGE AND WE BECAME empty nesters, Ed announced that it was a good time for us to get involved in church ministry. This was amazing on so many levels. For many years, although Ed professed God as his Creator and Jesus as his Savior, he had very little to show that he had wholeheartedly made Christ Lord of his life. I (Angie) had prayed for nearly eighteen years for Ed to take his role as the spiritual leader of our family more seriously. I had also prayed for him to be more understanding and supportive of my desire to be involved in Bible studies and women's ministry. It seemed like my involvement caused more friction than spirituality in our relationship. By the time Ed made his announcement, I had given up dreaming that Ed would get involved in ministry, although I secretly mentioned to God a time or two that with all of Ed's gifts if He ever *did* get involved, he was someone God could use mightily.

So, I was shocked when Ed announced that day that we should explore ministries. But I shouldn't have been. Ed had been showing signs of spiritual growth by attending church more regularly and encouraging us to get baptized as a family. I had so resigned myself to the idea that Ed was not going to take his role as the spiritual leader more seriously that I was blind to how God had been working on his heart.

At that time, we were attending Saddleback Church in Lake Forest, California, which Dr. Rick Warren pastored. Kathy Jo Stones, the new Director of Pastoral Care, had recently started a premarital counseling ministry. One of her biggest challenges was leading the church lay counseling ministry of over 100 counselors. When she came on staff, lay counselors did the premarital counseling—one individual lay counselor working with each premarital couple. She tells the story:

> *One day I sat in while a premarital couple was being counseled. Even though the counselor was astute and intuitive, he was not a married man, nor was he trained in the specific issues related to premarital couples. After observing this dynamic, I envisioned the possibility of married couples counseling premarital couples. I imagined the married couple being trained explicitly to work with premarital couples, establishing a mentoring relationship, and using their years of marriage experience.*

With her passion for building strong marriages, Kathy Jo masterfully crafted a unique premarital counseling program in which mature Christian married couples mentored engaged couples for six weeks. The ministry was an immediate success.

Introduction

We (Ed and Angie) thought it would be fun to engage in a ministry we could do together, so we attended one of the earliest training classes Kathy Jo taught. She had compiled materials from numerous resources. As great as the program was, the materials were a little cumbersome and confusing. They did not complement the outstanding program she had launched. Ed has excellent organizational and business skills, so a few months later, he approached Kathy Jo and offered our services to research and write material tailored to the program format. He envisioned making it concise and friendly yet still comprehensive. We read, researched, and keenly observed everything we could for a year to produce the curriculum that Saddleback Church has used since 2002. Churches throughout the world now use the curriculum.

> We initially became involved in this ministry to give back to God, but we quickly learned we could not out-give God. After just a short time in this ministry, God blessed our relationship and made our good marriage better than we ever dreamed possible. Mentoring others on the principles of living a Christ-centered marriage blessed our marriage with a oneness we had never experienced before. Today, we have a fantastic relationship. It is not perfect, but there are far more ups than downs. Even better, the ups are higher, and the downs, not so low. The downs get back on track within a few minutes or hours instead of days. We continue to grow every year in new and exciting ways.

And we are not alone. The other Marriage by God mentors experienced this same blessing in their marriages.

Little did we know that the Premarital Counseling Ministry at Saddleback Church was going to be just the beginning of the journey on which God would take us. He showed us repeatedly that we pray too small and that God is much bigger than we believed.

God opened doors for our premarital program to spread abroad to the Philippines, China, India, Singapore, New Zealand, Argentina, Brazil, and Russia. He provided opportunities for us to share our passion in all-day conferences in the Philippines and Singapore. Through some remarkable circumstances, he even had us share Christian marriage principles with a secular audience at the TEDx talks in Albany, New York.

God also took Kathy Jo on an incredible journey. Her passion for counseling—especially couples—grew during her years at Saddleback. To continue developing her skills, she went back to school for a graduate degree in clinical psychology, with an emphasis on marriage and family therapy. In 2007, she received her Marriage and Family Therapist license. She had a thriving private practice in Mission Viejo until her retirement in 2021. She has returned to Saddleback Church as a volunteer who supervises interning therapists. Working with couples is her passion and specialty.

WHAT TO EXPECT

This personalized curriculum guides you through sound biblical teachings, great discussions, challenging principles, and fun exercises. A mature Christian couple will mentor you through six sessions. They are not professional counselors, nor do they have a perfect marriage. However, they do possess numerous years of marital experience, and they have encountered many of the same problems and issues you may experience in your marriage. They have a passion for living out a Christ-centered marriage and helping others navigate doing the same. They are involved in this ministry to live out loving God and loving others. Your mentor couple's goal is not to solve problems for you but to equip you with the tools necessary to solve your problems. As the old saying goes, "Give a man a fish, and you feed him for a day; teach a man to fish, and you feed him for a lifetime."

> As you start the workbook, please remember that the more honest and open you are with your answers, the more you will learn from the program. The effort you put into this program will come back to you exponentially!

Please complete each session's lessons before you meet. Please complete the workbook separately from your fiancé. Please do not discuss the chapter or answers with your fiancé before your session.

HERE ARE A FEW SUGGESTIONS THAT WILL MAKE YOUR EXPERIENCE MORE ENJOYABLE AND BENEFICIAL

- Arrive on time.
- Go into your sessions with an open and positive mind.
- Come prepared to meet for approximately two hours.

Studies show that the happiest people in the world are married, but sadly, the unhappiest people in the world are also married. This program aims to take you on a journey to become one of the happiest couples. As you can see, the stakes are high, and the goal is lofty, but we want you to understand what it is to be one of the happiest married couples!

Let's get started!

NOTES

SESSION ONE

TWO BECOMING ONE

For this reason, a man will leave his father and mother and be united to his wife, and they will become one flesh — Genesis 2:24

IN 1978, ANGIE AND I BLISSFULLY WALKED DOWN THE AISLE TO BEGIN our lives together as one. Angie was just 19 years old, and I was 26. Although we would have called ourselves Christians—we both acknowledged God as our Creator and Christ as our Savior—neither one of us really knew what it was to fully surrender and make God Lord of our lives. We both felt committed to living good moral lives to the best of our abilities. Angie felt compelled to follow the "good Christian way" of going to church every Sunday. Since I had to work many weekends, I thought that she could cover the spiritual base for our family most of the time.

We settled into marriage. A few years later, we started our family. Our oldest son, Casey, arrived in 1981, followed by his younger brother, Corey, just thirteen months later. Instead of going back to work full-time after our second son was born, Angie worked alongside me in our real estate business. As the stresses of family and work mounted, so did the strain in our relationship. We learned to make things work, but it seemed as if we were more like great roommates than husband and wife. Things weren't horrible: they were just a lot less than either one of us had expected in our marriage.

Before we married, we went through premarital counseling classes taught by an unmarried pastor to a classroom full of engaged couples. We learned a few things, but we were not equipped with practical tools to draw on as we entered our marriage. Most marriages go from "I do" to "What do I do now?" We were that couple. We were still very much in love, but we had no idea how to live the married life we had both dreamed about.

> It was twenty years into our marriage before we learned practical skills for operating as a team and how to put Christ at the center of our marriage. We will take you on a journey to acquire some powerful tools to live out God's design for your marriage.

Authors Note: Throughout this book, the names have been changed in the stories involving premarital couples.

Session One | Chapter 1 | Two Becoming One

LET'S GET STARTED WITH SOME FOUNDATIONAL CONCEPTS

From the very beginning, God wanted a husband and wife to operate together as a singular unit. Genesis 2:24 states, "For this reason, a man will leave his father and mother and be *united* to his wife, and they will become *one flesh*" (emphasis added). The Hebrew word used for united, *dabaq*, means "to cling, cleave, keep close, stick to, or adhere to" (like glue). So, we can think of marriage as being "glued together as one." And as Jesus firmly states, "Therefore what God has joined together, let man not separate" (Mark 10:9). That sounds pretty permanent!

God intends for the husband-and-wife relationship to be uniquely united in a oneness unlike any other earthly relationship.

For a husband and wife to truly stick together as one flesh the way God intends, they must submit to the leading of the Holy Spirit in their relationship. The Holy Spirit is the glue that unites them together as one. If this is difficult to comprehend, it is with good reason: Ephesians 5:31–32 expands the verse in this way, "'For this reason a man will leave his father and mother and be united to his wife, and the two will become one flesh.' *This is a profound mystery*" (emphasis added). God intends for the husband-and-wife relationship to be uniquely united in oneness, unlike any other earthly relationship. This is a mystery that can only be accomplished when a couple recognizes the covenant of being joined together by God and is submitted to the leading of the Holy Spirit.

> One of the foundational ideas that differentiate a secular marriage from a God-centered marriage is that a God-centered marriage assumes a union of three: God, husband, and wife. Ecclesiastes 4:12 says, "Though one may be overpowered, two can defend themselves. A cord of three strands is not quickly broken." A cord or braid appears to contain only two strands, but it is impossible to create a braid with only two strands. When two strands are wrapped together, they quickly unravel. Herein lies the mystery: What looks like two strands requires a third. The third strand, though not immediately visible, keeps the strands tightly woven.

In a Christian marriage, God's presence, like that third strand in a braid, holds the husband and wife together. As a couple, one of the most important steps towards creating a solid marriage is placing God as the leader. As you enter marriage, submit to God being Lord of your lives and Lord of your marriage. Acknowledge the need to have God in control of all your decisions, directing and leading every aspect of your lives.

COMPLETE THE QUESTIONS ON THE FOLLOWING PAGE

Session One | Chapter 1 | Two Becoming One

*Please answer all the following questions independently of your fiancé.
Do not compare answers until you meet with your mentors.*

1. Give at least three advantages to being married over being single.

2. What would you like to see God accomplish through this premarital mentoring program? Be specific.

3. Have you had a breakup anytime since you became exclusive? If so, what was the reason?

4. How do you feel about divorce?

5. On a scale of 1 to 10, rate your compatibility in the seven areas below.
   1 = not compatible at all   10 = extremely compatible

FACTOR	RATING	FACTOR	RATING
Fun		Forgiveness	
Friendship		Future	
Finance		Faith	
Family			

Together Forever | God's Design for Marriage

SESSION ONE

Chapter 2

LOVE SPOKEN HERE

God is love — 1 John 4:8

WE WILL NEVER FORGET A DISCUSSION MANY YEARS AGO AT A DINNER with two other married couples. Ed shared a study he had read that concluded if you kiss your wife good-bye every morning and tell her you love her, you will not only have a better marriage, but you will also live five years longer and make 20 percent more income than those who do not. Whether or not the study had merit, it certainly led to some lively discussion that evening. I (Angie) started by saying that Ed is excellent about kissing me good-bye every morning, even when he is leaving at 5:30 a.m. to play basketball. I also said that he is the *best* at saying "I love you" to me throughout the day. Then Karen said that her husband Dan was also great about kissing her good-bye and telling her often that he loves her. At this point, Lisa sadly turned to her husband, Rob, and said, "Rob, you never tell me you love me." Rob looked at Lisa and said, "I told you I loved you before we got married. If I ever change my mind, I will let you know." We all laughed—all of us, except for Lisa. Rob's failure to communicate his love to Lisa had caused deep hurt.

That simple little word *love* profoundly impacts a marriage. Therefore, it needs to be communicated in words and actions daily.

When the two of you come together on your wedding day, it will be evident to your family and friends that you are in love. However, *love* is hard to define, perhaps because there are so many types of love but just one English word to describe them. For example, we say we love our fiancé, we love our children, we love our car, and we love ice cream. We use the same word, "love," with very different meanings in all these examples. To help us differentiate, we'll use three words the ancient Greeks used for love: *eros*, *philia*, and *agape*.

EROS • ROMANTIC, SENSUAL, OR SEXUAL LOVE

In a sexually fulfilling marriage, a husband and wife will be physically attracted to one another and love each other romantically. Eros is the root of the word *erotic*, which means "to arouse sexual desire or excitement."

PHILIA • FRIENDSHIP LOVE

True friendship exhibits attributes like loyalty, accepting you for who you are, honesty, and trustworthiness. The person you marry should hold a special place as your very best friend. Philadelphia, the city of brotherly love, takes its name from this word.

AGAPE • OFTEN REFERRED TO AS UNCONDITIONAL LOVE, BUT IT IS SO MUCH MORE

Agape love is sacrificial, unconditional, absolute, and always forgiving. Agape love in marriage tells us to deny ourselves and to put our spouse first. It is selfless. It always wants what is best for the other person. In marriage, agape love is not something that just happens. It is not a feeling. It is an act of the will even when we are not feeling love towards the other person. God's love for us is agape.

> *If you look at your fiancé through God's eyes, you will see him or her differently.*

Marriage is the only relationship God fashioned to experience all three types of love. The oneness that God designed for couples to share in marriage is a product of eros, philia, and agape love working together continuously in the relationship.

In the coming chapters, we will look more closely at eros and philia love. In this chapter, we will explore agape love. We will also see how God's agape love is a model of how we should love God, our spouse, and others.

Agape love, or selfless love, usually runs contrary to our selfish, sinful nature. In marriage and other relationships, we want our own needs met. We want to feel good about ourselves and protect our rights. This is contrary to God's ways. He wants us to put ourselves aside and place Him (God) first and others second. When asked which commandment was greatest, Jesus said, "'Love the Lord your God with all your heart and with all your soul and with all your mind and with all your strength.' The second is this: 'Love your neighbor as yourself.' There is no commandment greater than these" (Mark 12:30–31). When we follow these commands and love others in this way, we glorify God.

To love others with agape love, we need first to receive and experience God's love ourselves. Knowing how much God loves us allows us to love others more fully. First John 4:7–8 says, "Dear friends, let us love one another, for love comes from God. Everyone who loves has been born of God and knows God. Whoever does not love does not know God, because *God is love*" (emphasis added). God *is* love! Love is not just an emotion God created, but it is the full embodiment of God himself. God's love for us is always 100%. There is nothing we can do to cause Him to love us any more or any less. As you meditate on God's love for you, begin to reflect on his love for your partner. If you look at your fiancé through God's eyes, you will see them differently.

> If love in your relationship is ever feeling strained, go to love's source: God. Talk to Him in prayer and read His love letter to you. God sees us fail repeatedly, yet He is never impatient or unkind. God sees our wrongdoings, but He doesn't record them. His love is long-suffering, and His forgiveness is never-ending. God never gives up on us, and He wants us to love our partner in the same way. First Peter 4:8 says, "Above all, love each other deeply because love covers over a multitude of sins."

Remember, agape is not a feeling but an act of the will. Choose to act lovingly in obedience to God's commands, even if you do not *feel* loving towards your partner. Romans 5:3–5 says, "We also rejoice in our sufferings because we know that suffering produces perseverance; perseverance produces character; and character, hope. And hope does not disappoint us, because *God has poured out His love into our hearts by the Holy Spirit, whom He has given us*" (emphasis added). When you struggle with loving your partner, ask God to fill you with His love for your partner. Even if your partner does not respond to your love, you will draw into a more intimate relationship with God through your obedience.

> God never gives up on us,
> and He wants us to love our partner in the same way.

One Saturday night, I (Angie) sat in church, mad at Ed over an argument that had left me angry and hurt. At that time, my way of dealing with hurt was withdrawal, and I was on day two of giving Ed the cold shoulder and silent treatment. Author Lee Strobel (*The Case for Christ*) was the guest speaker, and it happened to be his twentieth wedding anniversary. So, as I sat there stewing, he began talking about love and marriage. Not exactly what I wanted to hear. He shared that for their anniversary, he was giving his wife a Top Ten List of the ten things he loved most about her. As I sat there, I began to think of all the things I loved about Ed. I quickly reached ten. As I did, God began to soften my heart. The hurt and anger dissipated. Then I thought, I bet I could come up with 100 things I love about Ed. Over the next few days, I kept adding to my list. By the end of the week, I presented a list to Ed of 100 Things I Love About You. When he began reading it, he gave me a big grin. As he continued, his face softened. When he finished, my big strong husband had a tear softly running down his cheek. He was truly touched.

I learned a valuable lesson that night. Our emotions reflect what we choose to focus on. When I focused on my hurt, I felt hurt and angry. When I focused on my love for Ed, I was filled with the love of God. I vowed that day to choose to focus on loving others, especially Ed, rather than concentrating on my self-centered, unmet expectations.

During the following year, Ed gave me a similar list, we gave our sons lists, and they gave us lists. Over the years, we have shared this story with others who have created lists for their loved ones and received terrific results. Sharing our loving thoughts in words is a powerful way to express our love. The list is also good to refer back to if you ever start to lose those loving feelings.

Another way to rekindle love in your relationship is to reflect on when, how, where, and why you first fell in love with your partner. If possible, reenact an early dating experience. Reminisce about the first time each of you told the other that you loved them. Put the same time, focus, and attention into your relationship as you did in the beginning.

Agape love is different than the kinds of love the world offers. Worldly love suggests each partner give 50/50. In other words, love equally—give only as much love as you receive. Agape love says give 100 percent even when your partner doesn't. In marriage, God desires both husband and wife to give 100 percent. Yet, we have seen cases in which one spouse fully committed to God's agape love was enough to turn the relationship around.

God beautifully illustrates His love and gives us a model for how we should love our partner:

> *Love is patient, love is kind. It does not envy, it does not boast, it is not proud. It is not rude, it is not self-seeking, it is not easily angered, it keeps no record of wrongs. Love does not delight in evil but rejoices with the truth. It always protects, always trusts, always hopes, always perseveres. Love never fails.* — 1 Corinthians 13:4–8

God's love *never* fails! Is this the kind of unconditional love you are committed to giving your future spouse?

I regularly ask myself, "What is the most loving thing I can do towards Ed at this moment?" Sometimes it might just be to simply say, "I love you." Another time it might be to do something extra helpful. Still another time, it might be to give him a ten-minute foot massage (even if I am exhausted). Love comes in a lot of forms: words, thoughts, and actions. But love needs to be expressed daily through words and actions to be felt.

God shows us how to love sacrificially through agape love. He wants us to put aside our selfish ways and put others first. When we are in a relationship with God, our goal is to glorify Him through our actions, thoughts, and words. Loving our partners with agape love, especially if they are not behaving in such a lovable manner, is one way that we demonstrate our obedience to His Word. Agape love brings glory to God. May you and your fiancé experience God's agape love in more profound ways than ever before as you join in marriage.

COMPLETE THE QUESTIONS ON THE FOLLOWING PAGE

Session One | Chapter 2 | Love Spoken Here

*Please answer the following questions independently of your fiancé.
Do not compare your answers until you meet with your mentors.*

1. Which of the three types of love needs the most growth in your relationship (eros, philia, or agape)?

2. How often does your fiancé tell you that they love you?

3. If you were having a bad day, how could you avoid taking it out on your fiancé?

4. Review the passage on love in 1 Corinthians 13:4–8. Which of the actions described in this passage may be challenging for you to show your fiancé? Why?

5. List ten things you love about your fiancé.

SESSION ONE

Chapter 3

THE FREEDOM OF FORGIVENESS

Forgive as the Lord forgave you — Colossians 3:13

WE WERE OUT TO DINNER WITH SOME FRIENDS. DURING THE EVENING, I thoughtlessly criticized Ed in a hurtful way. Not my proudest moment. As we got into the car to drive home, he expressed his disappointment. I told him I was sorry. He finished by saying, "I am going to be mad at you for three more minutes." We both started laughing. Ed had masterfully pointed out that I had wronged him but kept the exchange about the hurtful situation light.

Over time, we all wrong our loved ones, whether overtly or through omission. Forgiveness is essential—especially within the context of marriage. A marriage without forgiveness develops bitterness. However, when dealt with honestly and effectively, a painful situation that requires forgiveness can actually lead to a stronger, healthier marriage. It is our refusal to ask and extend forgiveness that tears a relationship apart.

People's inability to extend forgiveness will ultimately hurt them more than the person they are not forgiving. Clinging to unforgiveness is like taking poison, thinking it will hurt the other person. Understanding and accepting God's love and forgiveness for us enables us to love and forgive others. God's forgiveness, lovingly expressed within marriage, can bless the couple with a stronger, healthier relationship. This chapter will explore the biblical model of forgiveness, how to process through the bigger wounds, and how to move quickly through minor hurts.

God has given us the ultimate model of forgiveness through the sacrificial gift of His Son, Jesus Christ. Romans 5:8 says, "But God demonstrates His own love for us in this: While we were still sinners, Christ died for us."

The gift of salvation is by grace, not because we earned or deserved it. Jesus commands us to forgive others because God has forgiven us. God wants us to forgive using Jesus as our example. He wants us to extend grace and forgiveness to our partner, whether the offense is big or small, regardless of whether or not they repent.

God understands that forgiveness does not come naturally to us; nonetheless, He does not look lightly at unforgiveness. In Matthew 6:14–15, Jesus warns, "For if you forgive men when they sin against you, your heavenly Father will also forgive you. But if you do not forgive men their sins, your Father will not forgive your sins." When we truly understand God's forgiveness and love towards us, we cannot help but extend that to others.

Many years ago, a group of Amish families demonstrated their deep understanding of this teaching. On October 2, 2006, gunman Charles Roberts took children hostage in an Amish schoolhouse. He shot ten girls aged 6 to 13 before turning the gun on himself. Five of the girls died. In a powerful expression of forgiveness, the Amish families, who had buried their daughters the day before, attended the killer's burial service and hugged the widow and other members of the killer's family. Later, they even donated money to the widow.

Clinging to unforgiveness is like taking poison, thinking it will hurt the other person.

Forgiveness is first between God and us. God commands us to forgive even when we have done nothing to deserve the wrong done to us. C. S. Lewis refers to pain as the megaphone God uses to get our attention.[1] Sometimes there is a lesson that God is trying to teach us through our circumstances. God may be working on different lessons in you and your spouse through the same hurtful circumstance. Perhaps this poem sums it up best:

> *People are often unreasonable, illogical, and self-centered. Forgive them anyway…*
> *Give the world the best you have…You see, in the final analysis, it is between you and God;*
> *it was never between you and them anyway."*[2]

Struggling to forgive is not sin. Choosing to harbor unforgiveness is. As we endeavor to forgive bigger hurts, we'll process anger, sadness, and loss. It will likely take a great deal of time and effort to experience the many feelings associated with a betrayal or breach of trust. Neglecting or minimizing healing steps may cause a couple to miss the lessons God wants to teach them to make their relationship better.

> Perhaps the most disheartening situation requiring forgiveness is when the offense keeps recurring, and there is no remorse or repentance. We need to forgive intentional, unrepentant offenses, too.

God calls us to forgive those who have wronged us, but this does not mean that we must trust them. Mark 11:25 says, "And when you stand praying, if you hold anything against anyone, forgive him, so that your Father in heaven may forgive you your sins." Forgiveness and trust are two separate acts. Breached trust takes time to restore. Trust is earned back through consistent accountability over time. Genesis 37–50 tells the story of Joseph and his brothers. Joseph forgave his brothers for selling him into slavery. He recognized that what they had intended for evil, God had used for good. But when his brothers came back into his life, Joseph tested his brothers before trusting them.

---

[1] C.S. Lewis, *The Problem of Pain* (New York: Macmillan, 1962), pg 93.

[2] This poem is a modified version of "The Paradoxical Commandments of Leadership" by Kent M. Keith. Accessed January 8, 2015, from http://quoteinvestigator.com /2012/05/18/do-good-anyway/#more-3828.

If you need to rebuild trust towards someone, be patient and focus positively on their changed behavior. If the person is unwilling to change their behavior to restore trust, you may need to put boundaries or natural consequences in place to protect against future wrongs.

If you are the one who broke trust in the relationship, go out of your way to assure the other person that your behavior has genuinely changed. Be accountable.

Forgiveness and trust are two separate acts.

We pray that you will never have to experience a big wound in your marriage; however, there are times in every marriage when minor offenses happen. Perhaps your spouse forgets a promise or is late for an important event. Maybe your husband or wife forgets your birthday or wedding anniversary. You may get hurt by words that felt harsh. God wants us to offer forgiveness freely and apologize when we have done something wrong without expecting anything in return. In Matthew 18:21–22, "Peter came to Jesus and asked, 'Lord, how many times shall I forgive my brother when he sins against me? Up to seven times?' Jesus answered, 'I tell you, not seven times, but seventy-seven times.'" Jesus knew that we would need to forgive others, especially our spouse, over and over again. With practice, this will become easier and more natural.

TEN WAYS TO CULTIVATE A FORGIVING HEART

1. GIVE GRACE
We tend to judge others by their worst act and yet judge ourselves by our best intentions. We are usually quick to forgive ourselves and move past our shortcomings. Give your partner the same grace. Jesus said, "Why do you look at the speck of sawdust in your brother's eye and pay no attention to the plank in your own eye? …You hypocrite, first take the plank out of your own eye, and then you will see clearly to remove the speck from your brother's eye" (Matthew 7:3, 5).

2. COMMUNICATE
Sometimes what we perceive as mean-spirited is merely misconstrued, mistakenly personalized, or misunderstood. Lovingly communicate your hurt feelings to your partner and allow them to clarify. Then release your hurt to God. Honestly addressing your frustrations allows for understanding, whereas passivity usually causes frustrations to become pent-up and acted out in negative ways.

3. BE UNDERSTANDING
Try to understand the motivation behind what was done to hurt you. It has been said, "Hurt people often hurt people." Perhaps your partner did not deal with a given situation appropriately because they were hurting or insecure.

4. LET GO OF HURT

Although your partner may have done something sinful that hurt you, lack of forgiveness is sinful behavior, too. When we struggle with forgiveness, often it is because we are resisting giving up our right to be hurt, pout, or have our partner acknowledge our position. Sometimes, we want to respond or defend our position instead of just forgiving and moving on. Instead, we need to take the focus off ourselves and put it back on what God has done for us and what He asks of us. As Paul wrote in Colossians 3:13, "Bear with each other and forgive whatever grievances you may have against one another. Forgive as the Lord forgave you."

5. REFLECT ON POSITIVE ATTRIBUTES

When your fiancé has wronged you, it is always good to put it into perspective. Reflect on your fiancé's positive attributes. If you need help remembering, refer to the list you wrote of ten things you love about your fiancé (page 20).

6. STAY POSITIVE

When we don't forgive our partner, we allow negative thoughts to rent space in our minds.

7. FORGIVE AS GOD DOES

We will never have to forgive our partner as much as God has forgiven us.

8. PAY ATTENTION

It is good to remember that, at some time, we will also need forgiveness. But, unfortunately, quite often, the very thing that we have trouble forgiving our partner for is the same thing we will turn around and do to our partner in a slightly different way. For instance, you may feel that your partner is critical of you in a specific area of your life; however, as you pay closer attention, you realize that you, too, are critical towards your partner in other areas.

9. SELF-REFLECTION

When something hurtful is said to you, there is often a grain of truth in it. Be open to examining your partner's words and consider how you might make some positive changes. Accept the lesson and release the hurt.

10. COMMIT TO FORGIVING

Commit to each other that you will never go to bed without forgiving one another, even if you must finish the discussion later.

We all need to forgive in many ways, many times throughout our lives, especially within marriage. God's command to forgive will take an act of the will and may or may not involve a repentant, remorseful spouse. Forgiveness may also involve a process of healing and restoration. Unfortunately, Satan would like to keep us in a state of unforgiveness. Don't give him that pleasure! When you struggle with forgiving your partner, go to the source of love and forgiveness—God. And remember, "the one who is in you is greater than the one who is in the world" (1 John 4:4).

COMPLETE THE QUESTIONS ON THE FOLLOWING PAGES

Please answer the following questions independently of your fiancé. Do not compare your answers until you meet with your mentors.

1. Why is it important to forgive your fiancé?

2. How do you forgive someone you are having trouble forgiving, and how do you know you have forgiven them?

3. When you forgive someone, must you also trust them?

4. Which of the mindsets for cultivating a forgiving heart will be most helpful going forward?

5. Is there anyone in your life you need to forgive, or from whom you need forgiveness? What is preventing forgiveness from taking place?

CONGRATULATIONS! YOU'VE FINISHED SESSION ONE

SESSION TWO

PUTTING CHRIST AT THE CENTER OF YOUR MARRIAGE

Jesus answered, "I am the way and the truth and the life. No one comes to the Father except through me" — John 14:6

FOR MORE YEARS THAN WE WOULD LIKE TO ADMIT, WE PURSUED OUR relationships with Christ individually, not as a couple. We went to church together, but we prayed, studied our Bibles, attended small groups, and ministered separately. When we finally started attending small group Bible studies together, talking about God's will for our lives and marriage, and especially praying together regularly, we grew deeper in oneness than ever before. We came to realize there is a big difference between putting Christ at the center of your individual life and putting Christ at the center of your marriage.

We believe there are many Christian couples like us out there. They both believe in God and regularly attend church together. Still they are afraid to get truly vulnerable with each other in prayer or deeply discuss matters of faith together.

The Bible (1 Corinthians 11:3 and Ephesians 5:23) tells us that the husband is responsible for being the family's spiritual leader. Although I (Ed) was successful in business and could speak at seminars to hundreds of people, I felt insecure about praying aloud with Angie. However, as I grew in my knowledge and understanding of God's Word, I came to understand the responsibility I was given as head of the house and began bringing the family together in prayer. I started small at first, gathering the whole family to pray together before going to church each Sunday. After getting comfortable with that, I began praying more often at regularly scheduled times and spontaneously when special prayers were needed. Finally, Angie and I started praying together, just the two of us, in an open, deep, and vulnerable way.

There is a big difference between putting Christ at the center of your individual life and putting Christ at the center of your marriage.

One day Angie said, "Most people view the act of sex as being the most intimate expression of love and oneness in marriage. I disagree. The most intimate act a couple can do is to pray together. In sex, you bare your bodies, but in prayer, you bare your souls." She was right. Today I understand that transparently praying together brings God into the oneness of marriage.

It puts you in tune with the leading of the Holy Spirit. So, when I decided to take my responsibility as spiritual leader seriously, the intimacy in our relationship intensified.

We were recently visiting with one of our past premarital couples that married about a year ago. Alyssa shared with us that she loved how intentional Jacob was about being a godly husband. She shared that as they crawl into bed at the end of the day, Jacob almost always asks about her day. Then he prays for her. She said, "It is *so* romantic. I feel so safe and loved. It melts my heart." Then Jacob piped in, "It's the best foreplay ever!"

A comment by Dr. Harold Sala states, "It's a fact, according to valid research: The greater a couple's spiritual commitment, the more satisfying their sexual relationship."[3] Another unique gift from God.

Transparently praying together brings God into the oneness of a marriage.

However, Jakob and Alyssa had some significant, unforeseen challenges in their first year of marriage that came from outside influences, but because they were so connected in prayer, they could face them together as a team, trusting God for the outcome. As a result, they had peace going through their difficulties, and God was faithful in answering their prayers in even more remarkable ways than they imagined.

LET US SHARE SOME OF THE GUIDES WE HAVE USED IN PRAYER

When we pray, we use simple, everyday language. We talk with God as though He were the third party in our conversation, sometimes even visualizing His presence by putting an empty chair in the room. In our conversation with God:

WE GIVE HIM *PRAISE*
The Bible tells us that God created all things for His glory. Psalm 150:6 says, "Let everything that has breath praise the LORD. Praise the LORD." Our praise brings God great pleasure.

WE GIVE HIM OUR *REQUESTS*
Prayer is powerful. Jesus tells us in John 15:7, "If you remain in me and my words remain in you, ask whatever you wish, and it will be given you." The Apostle John confirmed Jesus' words with this assurance in 1 John 5:14–15: "This is the confidence we have in approaching God: that if we ask anything according to His will, He hears us. And if we know that He hears us—whatever we ask—we know that we have what we asked of Him."

WE GIVE HIM OUR *THANKSGIVING*
In God's currency, asking and thanking are closely related. Philippians 4:6 says, "Do not be anxious about anything, but in everything, by prayer and petition, with thanksgiving, present

---

[3] Harold J. Sala, "Prayer Therapy and Marriage," *Guidelines Daily E-Commentary*, accessed February 21, 2007, https://www.guidelines.org.

your requests to God." We should cultivate a grateful heart and a thankful attitude toward God. We can begin thanking Him before we even receive His response. We have been amazed at God's answered prayers when our hearts were right towards Him.

WE GIVE HIM OUR *CONTRITE HEARTS*

Although all our sins are forgiven through what Christ did for us on the Cross, God still wants us to come before Him and repent with a contrite, broken heart. God wants us to turn away from our sinful behavior. We regularly pray for God to reveal any sin in our lives.

Several years ago, we started an annual tradition of each of us writing out a prayer for our marriage on New Year's Day and sealing it in an envelope. Then the next New Year's Eve, we would open our prayers and read them to each other. The first year we did this, I (Angie) wrote a very safe, conservative prayer. God answered every word of it. Ed, on the other hand, wrote a big, bold prayer. We were blessed to see that God answered his prayer too. From that time on, we both have made it a practice to pray boldly in God's will. After all, the Bible says, "You do not have, because you do not ask God" (James 4:2).

Just as prayer unites us in marriage, it is also essential to understand the unique roles God defined for husbands and wives and how these were meant to strengthen the union. The Bible says that God first created Adam from the earth. Then He created Eve from Adam. Woman's purpose is found in Genesis 2:18: "The LORD God said, 'It is not good for the man to be alone. I will make a helper suitable for him.'" God created Eve to be Adam's helpmate. God wants husbands and wives to work together as a team. In marriage, you are no longer two people who walk separately, concerned with getting your own way, but rather, two people who walk together in agape love as a team. Whereas in other parts of your life you may be placed to serve together with others, within your marriage, you are the only person who will have the role of husband or wife to your spouse. It is a unique position that God prepared for you alone.

> *God wants husbands and wives to work together as a team*

The Apostle Paul further defined the roles of husbands and wives when he wrote, "For the husband is the head of the wife as Christ is the head of the church" (Ephesians 5:23). Paul speaks of this hierarchical chain of responsibility in this passage too: "Now I want you to realize that the head of every man is Christ, and the head of the woman is man, and the head of Christ is God" (1 Corinthians 11:3). This chain of responsibility may seem challenging to understand. Yet, we see it every day in the workplace: most of us are responsible to a boss, and even CEOs are usually accountable to a Board of Directors and stockholders.

The role of the husband as the head of the wife in no way lessens her value. The Apostle Paul clarified this when he wrote, "There is neither Jew nor Greek, slave nor free, male nor female, for you are all one in Christ Jesus" (Galatians 3:28). Paul says that men and women enjoy equal status and privilege before God because of their position in Christ. However, equal status and marital roles are two different things.

The Holy Trinity (Father, Son, and Holy Spirit) is the perfect model for the way we should pattern ourselves in marriage. In her book, *The Excellent Wife*, Martha Peace explains it like this:

> *The Trinity is a relationship in which three eternal persons (each perfect and totally equal in being, power, and glory) reveal, know, and love each other tenderly and perfectly for the other's good. When they decide to set and accomplish a goal, God the Son and God the Holy Spirit, although equal, voluntarily subordinate themselves to God the Father in order to accomplish their perfect plans. As they work together, they are totally unified in desire, thought, and action until the goal's completion. Thus they are a plurality within a unity.*[4]

The Trinity operates as one with different roles. Here is how God instructs husbands and wives to do the same in Christian marriage:

> *Submit to one another out of reverence for Christ.*
>
> *Wives, submit to your husbands as to the Lord. For the husband is the head of the wife as Christ is the head of the church, His body, of which He is the Savior. Now as the church submits to Christ, so also wives should submit to their husbands in everything.*
>
> *Husbands, love your wives, just as Christ loved the church and gave himself up for her to make her holy, cleansing her by the washing with water through the word, and to present her to himself as a radiant church, without stain or wrinkle or any other blemish, but holy and blameless. In this same way, husbands ought to love their wives as their own bodies. He who loves his wife loves himself. After all, no one ever hated his own body, but he feeds and cares for it, just as Christ does the church—for we are members of His body. "For this reason a man will leave his father and mother and be united to his wife, and the two will become one flesh." This is a profound mystery—but I am talking about Christ and the church.* **However, each one of you also must love his wife as he loves himself, and the wife must respect her husband.** *— Ephesians 5:21–33 (emphasis added)*

Jesus modeled perfect submission to God the Father even though it was not easy. At the same time, He modeled perfect, sacrificial servant-leadership. This is God's desire and design for us in marriage. When the dynamics between a husband and wife are correct, their positive interactions will reflect honoring, praising, serving, loving, caring, trusting, and respecting one another. When the dynamics are incorrect, their negative interactions will reflect criticizing, nagging, complaining, blaming, and controlling.

> The roles of husbands and wives are not conditional. A husband is accountable to God for how he loves his wife, regardless of whether she respects and submits to him. Conversely, a wife answers to God for how she submits to and respects her husband irrespective of whether she agrees with his decisions or actions.

When God is at the center of our relationship, we can allow the Holy Spirit to work in and through us instead of just relying on our own strength. Therefore, regularly coming together in prayer as a couple is so important.

---

[4] Martha Peace, *The Excellent Wife* (Bemidji MN: Focus Publications, 1997), pg 30.

Session Two | Chapter 4 | Putting Christ at the Center of Your Marriage

IN ADDITION TO PRAYER, HERE ARE FOUR OTHER WAYS TO KEEP CHRIST AT THE CENTER OF YOUR RELATIONSHIP

1. JOIN A COUPLES' SMALL-GROUP BIBLE STUDY

2. GET INVOLVED IN A MINISTRY

God has given you and your fiancé a combination of opportunities and spiritual gifts that are uniquely designed for you. First Peter 4:10 states, "Each one should use whatever gift he has received to serve others, faithfully administering God's grace in its various forms." Pray and watch for God's leading in this area. He will place in your heart the direction He wants you to take. Consider whether there might be an area of ministry where your gifts would complement one another, and you could serve together as a couple. You'll be blessed if you live in God's will with your time, treasure, and talents. (If you find that you are overstressed with any of these, you are likely not in God's will.) When you are living out God's will for your life, two things will result: you will be blessed to be a blessing, and you will not be able to out-give God.

3. REMOVE ANY IDOLS FROM YOUR LIFE

Removing idols may seem like an odd concept, but God wants us to love Him with all of our hearts, minds, souls, and strength. Anything we put above God in our lives is an idol. We need to become more aware of what's on our mind, what we long for, what is important to us, and what we have our heart set on. It's not uncommon for jobs or ministry to become idols. Ironically, we can even make our spouses (or kids) idols in our lives because we are so intent on pleasing them. God should be our greatest longing and desire. We should set our thoughts, motives, and choices on trusting in and glorifying Him.

4. BE INTENTIONAL ABOUT SEEKING GOD'S WILL IN EVERY SITUATION, BIG OR SMALL

In order to follow God's will, we need to first know His will. Romans 12:2 says, "Do not conform any longer to the pattern of this world but be transformed by the renewing of your mind. Then you will be able to test and approve what God's will is—His good, pleasing, and perfect will." We can renew our minds through reading the Bible, praying, and seeking godly counsel from other mature Christians, but even then, our selfish desires and sinful responses keep us from staying in tune with God. We need to continually refocus our living day-by-day, walking step-by-step in His will through the guidance of the Holy Spirit.

This entire program focuses on putting Christ at the center of your relationship. Prayer is the greatest means for accomplishing this. Prayer acknowledges God's presence and softens our hearts towards one another. It is the perfect pathway to calm emotions when strife arises. It helps our wills conform to the roles God has given us in marriage. It releases the power of the Holy Spirit to help and guide us. When we share our deepest thoughts and emotions with our partner openly and honestly in prayer, we can emotionally unite in body, soul, and spirit the way God intended us to in marriage.

From the very start, God wants to be at the center of your marriage in every way. If you as a couple will make Christ Lord of all areas of your marriage, then you will know what it means to become one in Christ.

COMPLETE THE QUESTIONS ON THE FOLLOWING PAGES

Session Two | Chapter 4 | Putting Christ at the Center of Your Marriage

Please answer the following questions independently of your fiancé. Do not compare your answers until our next session.

1. Have you put Christ at the center of your life? If so, how?

2. **HUSBAND-TO-BE ONLY:** What does loving your future wife as Christ loved the Church mean to you?

   WIFE-TO-BE ONLY: What does submission to your future husband in a Christ-centered marriage mean to you?

3. Describe the kind of prayer life you want to have together when you get married.

4. How can your fiancé be praying for you right now?

5. How often do you read the Bible?

6. What sin in your life right now is keeping you from being closer to God?

7. What are ten things in your life for which you are thankful?

8. If you and your fiancé have a significant decision, what process would you use to ensure you will make a God-honoring decision?

SESSION TWO

Chapter 5

DEVELOPING AN INTENTIONAL MARRIAGE

The LORD will guide you always; He will satisfy your needs — Isaiah 58:11

A COUPLE USUALLY PUTS CONSIDERABLE EFFORT INTO THEIR relationship while they are dating and engaged. However, as they settle into marriage, they each have new expectations for their relationship. Many expectations in marriage come from our past experiences, attitudes, and beliefs. In addition, they originate from our parents, relatives, and friends. Your adjustment to marriage will be much easier if you both have realistic expectations and clearly discuss them with each other in advance.

God wants us to serve one another in marriage. Jesus gave us the perfect example of this when He humbled himself to wash His disciples' feet. Jesus even washed Judas's feet, and He knew Judas was about to betray Him. We need to follow Jesus' example and cheerfully, humbly serve our spouses with unconditional love. Agape love challenges us to serve and do it sacrificially, placing our spouse's needs above our own. "Serve wholeheartedly, as if you were serving the Lord, not men" (Ephesians 6:7).

If Jesus, being God, took on the role of a humble servant (even unto death), why should we think we can live our lives for ourselves?

Early in the marriage, we are eager to please one another, but after a while, it is easy to start seeing all the ways you are there for your spouse, but they fall short on meeting your needs. For us to demonstrate a Christ-like attitude in our marriage, we must change our motivation from "How can my spouse meet *my* desires?" to "How can I meet my *partner's* wants and needs?" We should love and respond with agape love by taking our focus off of ourselves. If Jesus, being God, took on the role of a humble servant (even unto death), why would we think we should live our lives for ourselves? Instead, we should each seek to glorify God with our life by having a servant's heart towards our spouse regardless of how they behave with us. We don't naturally default to having a servant's heart. We need to be intentional about it.

About eight years ago, Ed came up with an idea that demonstrates how to intentionally serve one another in love. He suggested that we start a weekly tradition of being king or queen for the day. This little exercise helps us understand and better communicate how we can each meet the other's needs and desires.

We started by each choosing which day of the week would be our special day. I (Angie) chose Friday. So, every Friday, I get treated like royalty. Ed wakes me up with a nice back rub; he warms my towel in the dryer and hands it to me as I exit the shower; he washes my car and fills it with gas; he sends me loving texts throughout the day. Saturday is Ed's day to be king. On Saturday, I treat Ed like royalty. I wake Ed up with a back rub; bring coffee to him in bed; surprise him with sweet little love notes throughout the house; give him a head massage; run errands for him; make him his favorite dinner. We both look for other special things to do for each other throughout the day.

At first, it was hard for me to tell Ed what I would like on my special day. I had a hard time feeling worthy. But, over time, I realized that when we both give and receive, a closer, more loving intimacy grows in our relationship. Today we have fun coming up with new and creative ways to treat each other on our special days. The best outcome has been that this exercise ensures that if our relationship gets offtrack, we will be back on course by Friday and Saturday.

As a couple gets comfortable with one another, it is common that they begin to take each other for granted. This is where the relationship had drifted with Kevin and Michelle who were going through Marriage Mentoring with us. They had been married for nine years and had two adorable little girls. As we waited for Michelle to take a restroom break, I (Ed) casually asked Kevin, a successful financial advisor, his secret to finishing No. 1 in his organization year after year. He said, "I get that question quite often from other people in my industry. It is simple. I treat every client as if they were Bill Gates. Good customer service is not enough. I create an *exceptional* client experience." Ed then asked him a follow-up question. "What would your marriage be like if you got up every day trying to make that day exceptionally special for Michelle?" He responded thoughtfully, "Great question." Michelle returned and our session continued.

Several weeks later, after they completed the program, Kevin and Michelle invited us over for dinner. After a delicious meal and as we enjoyed dessert, I asked Kevin what impacted him the most from the marriage enrichment program. He responded, "When you asked me what my marriage would be like if I worked on it as hard as I did my business. It was like a switch flipped. I finally realized if I wanted my marriage to be successful, it required intentional effort. Before I realized it, Michelle responded by going out of her way to do extra special things for me, too. It was like we were both trying to outdo the other with our loving actions."

> When our loved ones fall short in meeting our needs, how we choose to respond will either bring us closer together or drive us apart. We cannot control our partner's actions or responses. We can only control our own. The best way to react is to choose answers honoring God rather than responding to our partner in a hurt, angry, or passive-aggressive way.

Session Two | Chapter 5 | Developing an Intentional Marriage

HERE ARE THREE WAYS TO RESPOND WHEN YOUR PARTNER DOESN'T MEET YOUR NEEDS

1. BE CERTAIN THAT YOU HAVE HONESTLY, LOVINGLY, AND CLEARLY COMMUNICATED YOUR DESIRES TO YOUR PARTNER

Do not assume that your partner can read your mind and knows what you expect or need.

2. DETERMINE IF YOUR EXPECTATION IS REASONABLE

Unrealistic expectations are often fueled by our culture and cause disappointment and discontentment. When your expectations aren't appropriate, the best action is to lower them. People with reasonable expectations are happier than people who demand a lot of themselves and others. Demanding people spend much of their lives being disappointed. They tend to either hurt their relationships by nagging and dwelling on disappointments or suppress their emotions while feeling sorry for themselves. This self-absorption cultivates bitterness. Sometimes the most loving thing you can do is lower your desires and fill your mind with grace and unconditional, agape love towards your partner.

3. TURN YOUR UNMET EXPECTATIONS AND NEEDS OVER TO GOD

If you feel your partner is falling short of living out God's will in your relationship, take your disappointments to God. Ask God to work in your partner's life. Ask God to help you to love your partner with His unconditional love. Ask God to fill your needs when your partner is unable or unwilling. The Word of God tells us that Jesus Christ is sufficient to meet all our needs. Philippians 4:19 promises, "And my God will meet all your needs according to His glorious riches in Christ Jesus." Instead of living with the disappointment and discouragement of unmet expectations and needs, we can look to God and His Word to fill our lives. God will never disappoint or fail us. When we learn to release our unfulfilled desires to God (and make them between God and us, instead of our partner and us), God can fill us with His joy and contentment. Surrender to God your resentment, your disappointments, and your frustrations. Remember that only God is perfectly reliable. Just as you are imperfect, so is your mate. God is still at work in both of you!

It is best to accept instead of expect in order to have fewer disappointments and hurts.

Earlier in this chapter, we shared how Kevin realized that he would never imagine his business success without intentional effort. Yet, he was not putting as much effort into his marriage as he was into other aspects of his life. When he finally did, his marriage flourished. One of the greatest gifts you can give your fiancé as you enter into marriage is to develop a lifelong intentional attitude of serving your partner in love.

COMPLETE THE QUESTIONS ON THE FOLLOWING PAGES

*Please answer the following questions independently of your fiancé.
Do not compare your answers until our next session.*

1. On a scale of 1-10 (10 being the best), to what extent does your fiancé currently meet your needs in each of the following areas?

NEED	RATING
Admiration towards you	
Affection towards you	
Conversational needs	
Family connectedness	
Financial security	
Honesty and openness	
Help with chores or errands	
Recreational activities together	
Maintaining attractiveness	

2. How can your fiancé be more intentional about meeting the needs you outlined above?

3. What are some of the desires for your future marriage that your fiancé may not be aware of?

Session Two | Chapter 5 | Developing an Intentional Marriage

4. If your partner doesn't meet your expectations and needs, how should you respond?

5. List 5 steps can you take to assure you live an intentional marriage.

6. If, one day, your fiancé says, "You are going to be king/queen for the day. Give me a list of 5 special things I can do for you today," what items would you list? Also, what day of the week would you like your king/queen day to be?

SESSION TWO

Chapter 6

FINDING THE SWEET SPOT IN YOUR RELATIONSHIP

And there will be harmony between the two — Zechariah 6:13

WE LIKE TO SAY THAT A JOYFUL RELATIONSHIP IS LIVING IN THE "sweet spot." A couple is in the sweet spot when they feel connected in all areas—emotional, physical, spiritual, and social. Everything is flowing in a positive way. Interaction is pleasant, happy, kind, and loving. There is harmony in the relationship. They are operating as a team, as one. We call the opposite of the sweet spot the "sour patch." This is when the connectivity or oneness has been disrupted.

During a mentoring session, Brandon mentioned that it seemed his relationship with Mandy was great most of the time; however, when they argued, it would sometimes take days or even weeks for them to get over it. Brandon and Mandy are both very bright, but they had no answers when Ed asked what steps they could take to get back into their sweet spot. They just let things take their course and waited it out. Brandon and Mandy's situation is very common. They had love and commitment towards one another. They simply lacked the tools to get their relationship back on course when it got offtrack.

Relationships tend to have a momentum that moves them in either a positive or negative direction. This is especially true in marriage because a couple's lives are intimately intertwined. When a marriage starts to spin in a negative direction, it takes an intentional effort to stop that momentum and get it moving back in a positive direction. There are specific skills and time-tested techniques that, when either a husband or wife implements it into their marriage, can shift the relationship back into the sweet spot. This chapter is about helping you understand some of these tools.

When a marriage starts to spin in a negative direction, it takes an intentional effort to stop that momentum and get it moving back in a positive direction.

Session Two | Chapter 6 | Finding the Sweet Spot in Your Relationship

The following is a list of nineteen practical tools. Some are for keeping your relationship in the sweet spot, while others are for helping you get back into the sweet spot. You may notice that some of these ideas have been explained in previous chapters, and some are new.

This chapter has only three questions. In addition to answering these three questions, we want you to come prepared to explain each of the ideas presented here. This chapter teaches skills that can make a life-changing difference in your relationship as you join in marriage. Please do not cut corners—take time to grasp these concepts.

TOOLS FOR STAYING IN THE SWEET SPOT

1. PRAYER

When a couple has drifted into the sour patch and humbly comes before God together in prayer, they are more receptive to setting aside their individual agendas and selfish desires. Instead, they are open to seeking the will of God, who loves them and wants them to operate as one. Imagine how healing it would be to pray as a couple when things start to enter the sour patch. This is an excellent step for the man to initiate as the spiritual leader of the family, although a woman can always suggest praying together, too.

2. "I'M SORRY. I WIN!"

Use this tactic to take advantage of your competitive nature and make a game out of forgiving quickly. Whoever says they are sorry first wins! Now instead of letting little things fester, if one of you will promptly say sorry (knowing they just won), you can move forward with a smile. It's a great way to solve a problem and win at the same time. For example, one day Angie and I (Ed) had cross words just as I was getting ready to leave for a meeting. Just after I left the house, I received a text from Angie that read, "I'm sorry." A few seconds later, I received a second text that read, "I win!" It made me laugh, and we were quickly back in our sweet spot.

Fun is the litmus test for a good marriage.

3. FUN

For the health of your relationship, it is essential to keep fun alive, but this is an area that will disappear when you are in the sour patch. Even if you are not feeling it, plan something fun that you both will enjoy doing together. The simpler, the better. Some couples like going back to doing something they enjoyed when they first dated. Couples should be able to bring out the playful child in each other. Laughter should flow freely. It has been said that fun is the litmus test for a good relationship. Good marriages have fun, and marriages that have fun are good.

4. MAD FOR FIVE MINUTES

There are times that you would like to let your fiancé know that you are a bit upset, but you don't want to make a mountain out of a molehill. An effective way to communicate your displeasure to your fiancé and still keep things in perspective is to say, "I am going to be mad at you for five minutes." You both may laugh at the comment, but the point will have been made.

5. ACT OF KINDNESS

Doing a loving act of kindness towards your fiancé when you are not feeling it is a great way to let your partner know how committed you are to getting back into the sweet spot.

6. LOVE GRAFFITI ON THE MIRROR

Use a dry-erase marker to write a love note to your fiancé. Keep an assortment of dry erase markers in your bathroom so you can be creative with your messages.

7. "HOW FULL IS YOUR LOVE TANK?"

Ask your fiancé, "On a scale of one to ten, how full is your love tank right now?" Follow up by asking, "What would it take to make it a ten?" (This one is perfect for us guys because it comes with instructions).

8. REPLACE A CRITICISM WITH AN AFFIRMATION

When you are tempted to criticize your fiancé, stop yourself and replace the critique with a genuine compliment. Criticism is one of the quickest ways to drive your relationship into the sour patch. By praising your fiancé, instead of making the situation worse, you'll make it better.

9. SMILE

A simple smile can change the entire chemistry between you and your partner. A smile will warm the heart of your fiancé. A smile makes you appear more attractive. Studies have shown that smiling reduces blood pressure, lowers stress, boosts your immune system, releases endorphins, makes you more positive, and builds confidence. Smiles are contagious, so be the initiator.

10. TEN THINGS I LOVE ABOUT YOU

In your first session, you each made a list of "Ten Things I Love About You." When you are drifting into the sour patch, pull these lists out and reread what you love about your spouse and what they love about you. Then, once your heart is softened, ask your fiancé to do the same. Now, each of you should add some new items to your list.

11. BIG PICTURE

When you and your fiancé argue, ask yourself, "In the scope of eternity, does this really matter? For the sake of our relationship, can I just let it go?"

12. TEXT

Sometimes a loving text is all it takes to get back into the sweet spot. Recently Angie's phone was nearing the memory limit, and she asked me to help her free some memory. So, I asked her if I could delete her text messages for the last two years. She said, "Yes, all except yours." She explained that occasionally she likes to go back and reread my loving text messages.

13. KING/QUEEN FOR THE DAY

You learned this in an earlier chapter. Hopefully, this is something you will incorporate into your weekly calendar. This is a relationship game changer. It brings your relationship into the sweet spot.

14. SPECIAL TIME

Special time is one-to-one connected time together. It is important to keep dating even after you get married. It doesn't have to be fancy or expensive. It just needs to be kept a priority.

15. "I LOVE YOU"

These words can be music to your partner's ears. Add a hug and a long romantic kiss for extra credit.

16. START ALL OVER

Occasionally you have a day that seems to go sideways from the start. When this happens, all it takes is for one of you to say, "Can we start over?" By prior mutual agreement, this is a pact to start over with no talk of what may have caused the day to go wrong in the first place. This cannot be used for significant problems but is an excellent tool for minor issues.

17. LOVE AND RESPECT

Women want to be cherished by their husbands, and men want to be respected by their wives. So, when you are married, continually do things to make your wife feel special and adored by you (especially in front of others). Let her know you are her protector and will keep her safe and secure. As a wife, continually show your husband you are on his team and his biggest fan. Believe in him and avoid questioning or correcting him in front of others.

18. MAKE IT BETWEEN YOU AND GOD

Make it between you and God instead of you and your spouse. Do the right thing because you want to be pleasing to God, even if you are not feeling it towards your fiancé at that moment.

19. GO OUT FOR ICE CREAM!

Michelle and Ron lost their sweet spot. They'd been married only eight months. They hadn't attended premarital mentoring and now felt significant stress in their relationship. Finally, they came to us and asked if we would mentor them. During our first session with them, it was clear that they were very much in love, but financial pressures from working multiple jobs to pay off their wedding debt were overwhelming them. They shared similar goals but had no fun in their lives. They couldn't remember the last time they laughed or had a good time together since their wedding.

At the end of a serious first session, I (Ed) gave them a homework assignment: go home and have a pillow fight sometime before the next session. When they arrived for session two, I asked them how their assignment went. They said at first it was very awkward. But they knew we would hold them accountable, so they had to do it. Once they got started, though, it wasn't long before they were laughing and giggling like kids. They eventually found themselves playfully wrestling on the floor. Michelle beamed as she said it was the first time they had enjoyed each other in months. With a little twinkle in his eye, Ron remarked that it led to some of the best sex since their honeymoon! They were still under the same financial pressures as the week before, but they had a renewed sense of oneness and harmony that made the everyday stresses manageable as long as they were connected. They were in their sweet spot again.

> Dwelling in your sweet spot builds momentum in a positive direction. Conversely, dwelling in negative feelings and interactions builds momentum in a negative direction. Either one of you can initiate the steps necessary to change the momentum to return your relationship to the sweet spot.

You may not use all these tools; however, choose some you identify with and become proficient at them. Of course, there will be times in your marriage when more significant problems will arise, and these steps will not be enough to get you back on track. In a future chapter on resolving conflict, we will share a plan of action to address more significant issues.

COMPLETE THE QUESTIONS ON THE FOLLOWING PAGE

Please answer the following questions independently of your fiancé. Do not compare your answers until our next session.

1. How would you define the sweet spot in your relationship, and when do you know you are in it?

2. You will be asked by your mentors to give a recap of the tools outlined in this chapter. Which tools mentioned are you most likely to use?

3. Share a memory of the two of you having fun together.

 CONGRATULATIONS! YOU'VE FINISHED SESSION TWO

SESSION THREE

Chapter 7

PERSONALITY DIFFERENCES

I praise you because I am fearfully and wonderfully made — Psalm 139:14

DURING OUR PREMARITAL COUNSELING, THE PASTOR ASKED EVERYONE IN the group to raise their hand if they were compatible with their fiancé. All twenty of us raised our hands high, only to have the pastor tell us we were all wrong. We were sure he was crazy. After all, we had known each other for eighteen months and were convinced we were perfect for each other in every way. The pastor explained that no two people are perfectly compatible but that a great marriage is not based on a man and woman being perfectly compatible, but instead on a husband and wife learning to manage their incompatibilities effectively.

Within just a few months of marriage, we knew what he meant. Instead of panicking and thinking we must have married the wrong person, we understood we needed to begin gaining skills to handle and cope with our incompatibilities.

Early in a relationship, couples often say, "We have so much in common," "We love the same things," and "We agree on almost everything." Once married, they say, "We are so different," "We don't understand each other," and "We can't seem to agree on anything."

You were attracted to each other's similarities and differences. You may have thought, "He will take care of our finances—he is more organized than I," or "She is more sensitive about others' needs than I am," or "He is more logical than I am about making decisions." Once married, these differences can become sources of friction. The differences that once seemed to attract now cause attacks. You think, "He is too controlling with the finances," "She is too sensitive about everything," or "He takes too long to make a decision." In other words, the differences that at first attract are what we later attack.

We are all created in the image of God. Yet, we are also each uniquely different. These differences are not right or wrong. The more we learn to embrace the differences we each bring into the marriage, the more we will understand how our different personalities complement and complete one another. God did not create any two people to be perfectly compatible. Our compatibilities (how we are the same as our fiancé), as well as our incompatibilities (how we are different from our fiancé), are both part of God's design for marriage. They draw us into the oneness that God intended for us in marriage.

One way we grew to better understand our personality differences was by taking the Myers-Briggs Type Indicator® (MBTI®) personality assessment instrument. I (Ed) am systemized and organized. I like to plan detailed specifics before proceeding. To me, early is on time. I want to finish projects ahead of schedule. I feel strongly that before I can permit myself to play, I need to complete all my work so that I don't have to return to unfinished work.

Differences are not right or wrong.

Angie, on the other hand, is happy to do her work and stop for play before the job is finished, even if it means she will have to work late into the night. Angie always had a hard time understanding why I put such pressure on myself. Likewise, I had difficulty understanding how she could play before getting her work done.

When we took the MBTI®, we both had "aha" moments. We saw that we each had very different personality types in respect to how we manage our lives. We became more understanding and accepting of our different styles. We realized we both accomplished everything we needed to get done. We just approach our tasks differently.

To further understand the personality differences between you and your fiancé, you can each take a personality test. There are numerous available online for free. We strongly encourage you to each take a test and discuss your results.

> God created you and your spouse with unique personality differences that reflect His image in each of you. These differences can help you accomplish more extraordinary things in marriage if you view your differences with respect and appreciation. Or these differences can cause marital discord if you view your way as the best or only way. Think in terms of operating as a team. A baseball team wouldn't function if every team member were a pitcher. The team needs different players with different skills to win the game. You both bring different skills, talents, and abilities into your marriage. Embrace these and operate as a team.

When your differences collide or become frustrating, talk honestly with each other. Speak gently, humbly, patiently, and lovingly. Allow these opportunities to draw you closer to each other and avoid letting resentment and bitterness develop. Above all, let God's grace and love prevail.

COMPLETE THE QUESTIONS ON THE FOLLOWING PAGE

Session 3 | Chapter 7 | Personality Differences

*Please answer all of the following questions independently of your fiancé.
Do not compare your answers until our next session.*

1. **Do you believe you and your fiancé are compatible? Explain.**

2. **The statements below reflect personality traits. On a scale of 1 to 10, describe how well the statement applies to you.**
   1 = does not describe at all   10 = very accurately describes me

NEED		RATING
A	I prefer to think things through carefully before moving in new directions.	
B	I enjoy being recognized publicly for my achievements.	
C	I generally don't like change.	
D	I have a daily to-do list and try to complete it.	
E	I am very spontaneous.	
F	I am very neat and tidy. I like things in their place.	
G	I am rarely late to an appointment, meeting, or event.	
H	I feel a sense of accomplishment when I complete a project. I am reluctant to start new projects until the ones I am working on are finished.	
I	I prefer socializing in small groups (ideally with just one other couple) rather than at big parties.	

To further understand the personality differences between you and your future spouse, you can take various online personality tests. One such test is located at http://www.16personalities.com.

SESSION THREE

Chapter 8

DIFFERENCES BETWEEN MEN AND WOMEN

So God created man in His own image, in the image of God He created him; male and female He created them — Genesis 1:27

DURING A PREMARITAL SESSION, BRANDT EXPRESSED HIS ANNOYANCE that his fiancé, Alexis, would often complain to him about her job. He would listen to her vent and then give her suggestions on how to resolve the issues. Instead of appreciating his help, she would shut down in frustration. Finally, he said in exasperation, "I don't get it. I get punished for trying to help." Angie, understanding the situation, asked Alexis, "How do you want Brandt to respond when you share your work problems with him?" Alexis responded, "I don't want Brandt to fix anything. I just need him to listen to me and maybe give me a big hug."

Men and women often feel misunderstood by their partners. It is natural for us to think that men and women function alike; however, that statement could not be further from the truth. The differences between men and women are extensive and wide-ranging. Just look at the titles of some of the books about the differences between men and women:

- *Why Men Don't Have a Clue and Women Always Need More Shoes:*
  The Ultimate Guide to the Opposite Sex

- *You Just Don't Understand:*
  Women and Men in Conversation

- *Men Are Like Waffles—Women Are Like Spaghetti:*
  Understanding and Delighting in Your Differences

- *Men Are From Mars, Women Are From Venus:*
  The Classic Guide to Understanding the Opposite Sex

> It's easy to see what a perplexing and challenging topic this is. Despite the notable gender differences, God created males and females equally and in His image. Together, men and women portray many of God's attributes. In simple yet profound ways, God designed our differences to complement each other, which ultimately enhances the oneness of the marriage relationship.

This chapter will look at some of the ways men and women differ. Of course, we can come to understand one another better through research, but it is good to remember that God's creation has many mysteries (including your future spouse) that have yet to be revealed!

GENDER DIFFERENCES

Dr. John Gray, author of the best seller, *Men Are From Mars, Women Are From Venus*, writes about the subtle differences between the brains of men and women:

> *Men's brains tend to perform tasks predominantly with the left side, which is the logical/rational side of the brain. Women, on the other hand, use both sides of their brains because a woman's brain has a larger corpus callosum, which means women can transfer data between the right and left hemispheres faster than men. …The other structural difference in men and women's brains is the limbic size, which controls bonding and nesting instincts.*
>
> *Females, on average, have larger, deep limbic systems than males. This is why Venusians [women] tend to be more in touch with their feelings and are better able to express them than men. The larger deep limbic system also increases a Venusian's [woman's] ability to connect and bond with others.*
>
> *The downside of this is that women are more susceptible to depression, not only because of the larger limbic system, but also because they produce less serotonin than men.*[5]

Thus, scientific evidence shows differences in the brain structures of men and women and, therefore, differences in their reactions.

Therefore, women typically are more relational, are more in touch with their feelings and the feelings of others and, are more nurturing than men. This means women are more likely to consider emotional ramifications when making decisions, while men typically consider logic.

You may have noticed this in your relationship. For most decisions, married couples benefit by looking at both emotional and logical perspectives. As you come together in marriage, the wife should be aware of the need to discipline herself to look at some decisions logically. Conversely, the husband should value the emotional perspective that his wife will contribute.

Since women and men process decisions and experiences differently (women relying more on emotions versus men relying more on logic), you'll need to put effort into communicating effectively. Using word pictures may help. For instance, a woman might say, "When we come together, I feel like a garden in full bloom, but when you criticize me for something, I feel like a wilted flower."

Jesus used word pictures when He spoke in parables. *The Language of Love: How to Be Instantly Understood by Those You Love*, written by Gary Smalley and John Trent, explains how to use word pictures to communicate your feelings more effectively.

Here are some common generalizations about males and females that can help you understand each other. However, just as there are differences *between* men and women, there are differences *among* men and women. Some of the differences described may not apply to your relationship.

---

[5] John Gray, "The Male vs. the Female Brain," *ThirdAge.com*, posted April 27, 2011, accessed June 23, 2012, http://www.thirdage.com/love-romance/the-male-vs-female-brain.

MALES TEND TO APPROACH A PROBLEM IN A MORE TASK-ORIENTED, "LET'S-FIX-IT" APPROACH

A man is more focused on solving the problem than on understanding the emotions associated with it. As a result, he will often decide based solely on the facts.

FEMALES TEND TO APPROACH A PROBLEM MORE CREATIVELY OUT OF SENSITIVITY TO AND CONCERN FOR THE FEELINGS OF THOSE INVOLVED

A woman speaks from her heart, describing in great detail the emotional aspects of the problem. By processing the situation and venting her frustrations to her husband, she feels connected to him. Unlike men, women don't always want — or need — to find a solution.

MALES TEND TO VIEW LIFE LINEARLY OR SEQUENTIALLY

A man wants to focus on one event, situation, or problem at a time. Men compartmentalize the different parts of their lives.

FEMALES TEND TO VIEW LIFE GLOBALLY

She can focus on multiple events, situations, or problems in an encompassing way. A woman tends to integrate the different components of her life and may handle all aspects simultaneously. She is more likely to carry emotions from one area into another.

MALES RELATE MORE SHOULDER-TO-SHOULDER

A man feels closer to others through sharing physical activities such as sports, hobbies, or tasks. He enjoys doing activities with his spouse, even if she is just there to observe. A man often feels closest to his wife after sexual intimacy.

FEMALES RELATE MORE FACE-TO-FACE

A woman is more interactive and relationship-oriented. She tends to focus on having meaningful conversations, building rapport, sharing experiences, and asking questions. A woman often feels closest to her husband after emotional intimacy.

MALES RECEIVE THEIR SELF-ESTEEM AND IDENTITY THROUGH CAREER SUCCESS AND APPROVAL OF WORK ASSOCIATES

A man desires respect and support from his wife. He wants his wife to be his No. 1 fan and operate as a team in marriage.

FEMALES RECEIVE THEIR SELF-ESTEEM AND IDENTITY FROM CLOSE RELATIONSHIPS, ESPECIALLY THEIR HUSBANDS

Even if a wife feels good about many areas of her life, she wants to feel cherished and special to her husband. A woman desires oneness in her relationship with her husband.

MALES DO NOT EXPERIENCE MONTHLY HORMONAL CHANGES

A man's role in the reproductive cycle—producing sperm—is not typically associated with emotional and physical symptoms.

FEMALES MAY EXPERIENCE MONTHLY HORMONAL CHANGES ASSOCIATED WITH THEIR MENSTRUAL CYCLE

Hormonal changes called premenstrual syndrome (PMS) typically begin five to eleven days before a woman starts her menstrual cycle. PMS refers to various physical and emotional symptoms, including mood swings, uterine cramps, food cravings, irritability, fatigue, and depression. A marriage benefits when a husband understands his wife's hormonal cycle.

Even if a wife feels good about many areas of her life, she wants to feel cherished by and special to her husband.

Some of the ways the differences between males and females will impact your relationship with your future spouse may surprise you. The mere fact that a man's brain is wired differently from a woman's brain means that men and women think, speak, relate, and make decisions differently. Not understanding sexual and hormonal differences can cause conflicts and disappointments. However, embracing your unique differences will allow you to operate together as the team God created you to be.

COMPLETE THE QUESTIONS ON THE FOLLOWING PAGE

Session 3 | Chapter 8 | Differences Between Men and Women

Please answer the following questions independently of your fiancé. Do not compare your answers until our next session.

1. How do you believe the general differences between men and women will affect your decision-making process in marriage?

2. Men and women arrive at their self-esteem in different ways. Taking this into consideration, how can you help strengthen your partner's self-esteem?

3. Men and women sometimes have different conversational needs. Has this created a problem in your relationship? If so, how? What solutions do you suggest?

4. Although men and women do not think alike, seeing things from your partner's perspective will help strengthen your relationship and create better teamwork. What are some ways you can suggest for learning and understanding what is important to your fiancé?

SESSION THREE

Chapter 9

LOVE LANGUAGES

Above all, love each other deeply, because love covers over a multitude of sins
— 1 Peter 4:8

INSIDE YOU IS AN EMOTIONAL LOVE TANK. IF IT IS FULL, THE WHOLE WORLD looks bright, and you dwell in your sweet spot. When your love tank is not filled by those most important to you, the world seems gray. If your love tank is half empty, you feel neglected and unloved.

> There are many ways to express and receive love. What speaks love to your fiancé may differ from what speaks love to you. Gary Chapman's book, *The Five Love Languages*, explores this topic. He says that the best way to love someone is to love them the way they want to be loved. In other words, speak to them in their love language.

We intuitively speak to our partner in the language we like to receive, which is not necessarily our partner's love language. This is like a boy buying his mother a football for Christmas. If you've ever received a different reaction from your partner than you expected when you said or did something thoughtful, this may be why. In your mind, you were expressing love, but since you were not speaking in your partner's love language, you did not make any emotional points. You can give yourself credit for trying, but this chapter's objective is to get you speaking fluently in your partner's love language so that their love tank stays full.

The first time we (Ed and Angie) taught this concept was with Heather and Ryan during their premarital mentoring. They lived an hour and a half apart. During this period in their relationship, their schedules brought them together only once per week when we met them for premarital mentoring. Heather was a task-oriented, high achiever. She had gone through college and obtained her MBA in just four years. As they came together each week, she gave Ryan a quick hug and kiss and then immediately asked Ryan if he had completed the task list she had given him for their wedding preparations. His joy in seeing her would immediately deflate. She would become disappointed when he had only gotten 75% through the list she gave him.

It was no surprise to learn when they took the Love Languages assessment that Heather's primary love language was acts of service. Ryan scored very low on acts of service. His primary love language was physical touch. Heather scored zero on touch (zeros are very rare). As they discussed their love languages test results, they shared how they had each experienced a draining of their love tank by the other: Heather, when Ryan didn't complete his list; and Ryan, when the list seemed more important to Heather than the two of them coming together affectionately.

Learning to speak in Ryan's love language was like giving me the key to his heart.

Six months after they wed, they invited us to see their new place and look at their wedding photos. As we enjoyed coffee and dessert, they cuddled on the family room floor and could barely keep their hands off each other. It was adorable and quite a change. We asked them what their favorite part of premarital mentoring had been. Heather immediately responded, "The love languages session. Learning to speak in Ryan's love language was like giving me the key to his heart." During that session, her eyes had opened to how important physical touch was to him. Heather had not grown up in a family that displayed affection through touch. She was genuinely enjoying this newfound expression of love. Ryan also realized that acts of service were important to her. Heather adjusted the lists she gave him to just a few things each day, and he dutifully made sure everything was accomplished. They had each learned how to keep the other's love tank full in ways that were at first not natural to them, and they grew closer than ever in the process.

> When you understand the concept of speaking in the correct love language, you'll find you can apply it to your family and friends and enhance those relationships, too (for other family members, you can access the Love Languages Test for free online at http://www.5lovelanguages.com). Moreover, you will find great joy in filling other people's love tanks. After all, "It is more blessed to give than to receive" (Acts 20:35).

BELOW IS A DEFINITION FOR EACH OF THE FIVE LOVE LANGUAGES

1. WORDS OF AFFIRMATION
Words of Affirmation involve providing honest, authentic, genuine, and focused compliments and positive, affirming words of encouragement. These help build another's self-image and confidence.

2. QUALITY TIME
Quality Time is shown by demonstrating how much someone means to you by setting aside special time with your full and undivided attention just being together, focusing on each other, and participating in shared activities and experiences.

3. GIFTS

Gifts of any type, large or small, express love to people who speak in this love language. The emphasis is on the thoughtfulness of the gift rather than the extravagance of the present.

4. ACTS OF SERVICE

Acts of Service are communicated by going out of your way to serve them by completing tasks joyfully. It is even more meaningful when action is taken without being asked. It shows that you genuinely care for, enjoy, and appreciate them.

5. PHYSICAL TOUCH

Physical Touch can be expressed through a simple touch on the shoulder, a gentle hug, or a passionate kiss. Physical touch is a powerful way to communicate your love for and comfort with someone.

LOVE LANGUAGE TEST

Please take the Love Languages Test at http://www.5LoveLanguages.com/quizzes or take the test that applies to you in the Appendices. "The Five Love Languages Test for Women" is in Appendix 3, and "The Five Love Languages Test for Men" is in Appendix 4. Enter your results in the table on the next page. Do not share your results with your fiancé until your next session. Finish by answering the three questions at the end of this chapter.

COMPLETE THE QUESTIONS ON THE FOLLOWING PAGES

Session 3 | Chapter 9 | Love Languages

Please answer the following questions independently of your fiancé. Do not compare your answers until our next session.

RESULTS TO LOVE LANGUAGES TEST

Count how many times you circled each letter and enter the result in the Letter Tally column. Add all results and confirm they total 30. Find the highest total and put a "1" in the Primary column to its right: that's your primary love language. Find the next highest total and put a "2" in the same column. That's your secondary love language.

LETTER	LETTER TALLY	PRIMARY	LOVE LANGUAGE
A			Words of Affirmation
B			Quality Time
C			Receiving Gifts
D			Acts of Service
E			Physical Touch
TOTAL:	30		

1. On a scale of 1 to 10, how full is your love tank?

2. What could your fiancé do to raise it to a 10?

3. Complete this sentence, "I feel most loved when …"

Use the three questions above to occasionally test how well you are meeting each other's needs and to know how you can better meet those needs.

CONGRATULATIONS! YOU'VE FINISHED SESSION THREE

NOTES

SESSION FOUR

Chapter 10

EXTENDED FAMILY

You shall rejoice in all the good things the LORD your God has given to you and your household — Deuteronomy 26:11

AS YOU COME TOGETHER IN MARRIAGE, YOU ARE EITHER LEAVING YOUR parents' home to live with your spouse or leaving the independence of living on your own to unite in marriage. Both scenarios require some adjustment. When you join together as one, you become each other's primary family. Your relationship with each other should now take priority over your family of origin.

I (Angie) was only 19 when I married Ed. I was the ultimate people pleaser who never wanted to disappoint my parents. As a result, whenever my family needed me for something or asked us to join them for an event, I would always say yes without checking with Ed. I always assumed Ed would understand and feel the same way I did. Fortunately, Ed was patient with me. As we approached our first anniversary, he lovingly pointed out that I wasn't treating him like he was the most important person in my life. I was shocked when I realized what I had done. I knew this was God's design for our marriage, but I had not been good about making the transition. I apologized to him. With this new awareness, I made the complete transition emotionally and mentally. I no longer put the wants or needs of my family of origin ahead of Ed. In my case, it was not my family who was putting pressure on me; I was just doing things as I had always done them. I can only imagine how hard this transition would have been had my family been putting pressure on me.

> The relationship dynamic between a husband and wife is challenging enough. When you factor into the equation the influences of parents, in-laws, and siblings (and sometimes blended family members), you can only imagine the friction that can result. Perhaps you are ready to make the transition to being each other's primary family, but your parents still want to view you as their primary family. Family obligations may cause stress between you and your spouse. If they do, establish some healthy boundaries. This may feel uncomfortable at first but will meet the overall goal of prioritizing your spouse.

Your family of origin will have more love, understanding, and forgiveness towards their own flesh and blood, so you need to be the one to establish the boundaries. Always approach them with love and respect, understanding that how you handle things will ultimately define your future relationship with your family.

Session 4 | Chapter 10 | Extended Family

The following discussion points will assist you in establishing a healthy relationship with your extended family that will complement your marriage. It will also allow you to have a fulfilling relationship with extended family members.

MAKE THEM FEEL SPECIAL

Establish a positive tone when you come together with family. Greet your family members in a way that makes them feel special.

BE POSITIVE

Speak positively about your spouse, and don't ever share marital problems with family members. It is easy to seek support from family members when you are frustrated, but after the conflict is resolved and you and your spouse have moved on, your family may have difficulty forgetting the hurt your spouse caused you. If you need to share marital frustrations with someone, choose one trusted, God-honoring, same-sex friend or seek professional church support.

UNITE

Face family challenges together. Unite with your spouse when making family decisions. Support your spouse in ways that will demonstrate your interest and care. Avoid minimizing, dismissing, or ignoring your spouse's concerns. Often, listening to your spouse's anger, disappointment, discouragement, sadness, or fear regarding family issues is the best action you can take. Be a safe person with whom your spouse can honestly share.

BE SUPPORTIVE

Support your spouse by being the one who delivers difficult or disappointing news to your own family, thus protecting the image your family will have of your spouse. This way, your spouse will continue to be viewed in a positive light. For example, suppose you cannot attend a family birthday party because of another prior commitment. In that case, the spouse whose family is being negatively impacted should be the one to break the bad news.

MANAGE EXPECTATIONS

You cannot control the way your extended family interacts with you and your spouse. However, you can manage the way you respond to them. Seek peace when disagreements occur.

ACCEPT

Accept that difficult extended family members may never change. Having high expectations of family members can lead to years of disappointment. The best predictor of future behavior is past behavior. To protect your heart, pray for God's love, grace, and forgiveness as you set appropriate boundaries.

The main point is to honor your spouse as a priority and your most important relationship, second only to God. When God blesses you with a life partner, you are being given a ministry to perform, that of glorifying God through your marriage. Therefore, make your marriage a priority.

COMPLETE THE QUESTIONS ON THE FOLLOWING PAGES

Please answer the following questions independently of your fiancé.

Do not compare your answers until our next session.

1. Genesis 2:24, "Therefore a man shall leave his father and mother and be joined to his wife, and they shall become one flesh." What does this statement mean to you?

2. Describe the relationship you have with your parents. How has this relationship shaped or impacted your view of marriage?

3. Do you ever share relationship problems with a family member?

4. How would you rate your relationship with your future in-laws on a scale of 1 to 10 (10 being best)? Explain.

5. What issues with your extended family might create a strain on your marriage?

6. Describe in detail where and with whom you will spend your first Thanksgiving and Christmas.

7. What can you do to express your love to your parents and future in-laws?

• *Be prepared to share a picture of your extended family at this session.*

SESSION FOUR

Chapter 11

COMMUNICATION

*Do not let any unwholesome talk come out of your mouths,
but only what is helpful for building others up according to their needs,
that it may benefit those who listen — Ephesians 4:29*

COMMUNICATION IS TO THE RELATIONSHIP WHAT BLOOD IS TO THE human body. It is vital, and it is life-sustaining. But just as human bodies become sick if a disease spreads to vital organs through the bloodstream, marriages become unhealthy if communication is infected with destructive practices. Effective, healthy communication is crucial to a thriving marriage.

> When couples struggle within their relationship, they often say they have poor communication skills. The fact is couples are continually communicating whether they realize it or not. A door slammed in anger, a sigh, a roll of the eyes, even the silent treatment are all ways we communicate. We send messages by what we *do* say and what we *don't* say. Unhealthy communication is not the problem as much as a symptom of the problem. In this chapter, we will discuss five components of healthy communication.

Communication consists of five components: content, tone, body language, timing, and listening. In other words, communication involves *what* we say, *how* we say it, the *body language* we use while saying it, *when* we say it, and *how* it is heard. So, let's look at each component and how each contributes to successful, loving communication.

We need to always be aware of how our tone of voice reflects criticism, blame, or sarcasm— all of these can be destructive to a relationship.

FIVE COMPONENTS OF COMMUNICATION

CONTENT

Content refers to the words we use to communicate our thoughts. Our words are the primary instrument we use to communicate quickly, effectively, and precisely. Many problems can arise with content. We may struggle with expressing our thoughts or feelings in the right words. Men and women differ in how they communicate content. You may think that you have communicated one thing while your partner has understood your words in a completely different way.

TONE

Tone refers to the volume and inflection we use when communicating. Tone can change the meaning of the content. It is the punctuation of our spoken word. (Imagine how difficult it would be to interpret the written word without punctuation.) Tone communicates many things, including enthusiasm, disinterest, and anger. Sometimes we find ourselves speaking in a volume or tone that seems inoffensive to us, but our partner perceives it as harsh. We need always to be aware of how our tone of voice reflects criticism, blame, or sarcasm—all of these can be destructive to a relationship. If your partner raises their voice, a good technique for de-escalating the volume is to lower your own voice: "A gentle answer turns away wrath, but a harsh word stirs up anger" (Proverbs 15:1). Try to be more aware of the tone you use in conversation with your partner and use it to reflect productive emotions like concern, care, support, and unconditional love.

BODY LANGUAGE

Body language refers to the position and movement of our bodies when we communicate. It is the form of language that is nonverbal.

> *One study at UCLA indicated that up to 93 percent of communication effectiveness is determined by nonverbal cues. Another study indicated that the impact of a performance was determined 7 percent by the words used, 38 percent by voice quality, and 55 percent by the nonverbal communication.*[6]

Body language is the form of communication that is most involuntary; therefore, it is usually the most honest. Nonverbal messages are communicated through gestures, postures, facial expressions, and other behaviors. You might not be a body language expert, but quite often, you can intuitively sense what others are saying through their nonverbal messages. Here are some body language tips you can use to communicate more positively:

- Make eye contact with your spouse when you are communicating.

- Use physical touch to express approval, care, concern, or support. A loving touch can help your partner feel safe in sharing their emotions.

- Study your partner's nonverbal communication. It may speak volumes to you—without even a word spoken.

- Be aware of what your nonverbal gestures are communicating, both negatively and positively. For example, are you expressing a loving, caring, and respectful attitude or a critical, defensive, unapproachable stance?

---

[6] Susan M. Heathfield, "How to Understand Your Coworkers' Nonverbal Communication," accessed May 23, 2019, https://www.thebalancecareers.com/tips-for-understanding-nonverbal-communication-1918459

TIMING

Timing refers to when you choose to communicate. You can be clear in content, tone, and body language, but if you select a poor time, you can be ineffective, or worse, communicate the opposite of what you intended.

During our mentoring session on communication with Matt and Kacie, Matt said that Kacie had a bad habit of dropping bombshells on him just as they arrived at church, so he wouldn't have time to respond. For example, she would save difficult news such as, "Oh, by the way, I know you wanted to watch the golf tournament today, but this afternoon was the only time I could set up for us to meet with the baker to taste cake samples for our wedding cake." This actually made matters worse because he not only received lousy news but felt sabotaged in the process.

There is truth to the saying, "Timing is everything." It is good to choose your timing wisely when communicating about sensitive issues. Choose times when you are not hungry, angry, tired, rushed, or preoccupied.

LISTENING

Listening is one of the essential components of effective, healthy communication. Everyone desires and needs to be heard. When couples don't listen to one another, the result is often frustration, anger, misunderstanding, and hurt. Poor listening skills can be an inherited family trait. Suppose you or your future spouse were raised in an environment where family members did not listen or were unable to express their feelings. In that case, you will likely have some challenges communicating and listening effectively. Don't be discouraged if this is true of your family of origin. You can change your past habits and build new patterns with effort and practice.

Good listeners listen with an open mind. They are careful not to judge their partner's feelings as right or wrong.

Communication expert Michael P. Nichols says, "Genuine listening means suspending memory, desire, and judgment—and, for a moment at least, existing for the other person."[7] Be alert to some common blocks to listening: judging, daydreaming, advising, reading someone's mind, filtering (selective listening), planning your response, and changing the subject (through blaming, being defensive, or being passive-aggressive).

Good listeners listen with an open mind. They are careful not to judge their partner's feelings as right or wrong. They are careful not to judge their partner's motives. They follow Paul's teaching to the Corinthians, "Therefore judge nothing before the appointed time; wait till

---

[7] Michael P. Nichols, *The Lost Art of Listening: How Learning to Listen Can Improve Relationships* (New York: Guilford, 1995), pg 64.

Session 4 | Chapter 11 | Communication

the Lord comes. He will bring to light what is hidden in darkness and will expose the motives of men's hearts" (1 Corinthians 4:5). Good listeners listen with their full attention instead of planning their response.

> One effective way to communicate that you are listening is to paraphrase to your partner what you have heard. This is called *reflective listening*. The Bible says it best: "Everyone should be quick to listen, slow to speak, and slow to become angry" (James 1:19).

As a married couple, there will be times when you will need to communicate a hard truth to your spouse. Accountability is crucially important in our battle against sin. Proverbs 27:17 says, "As iron sharpens iron, so one man sharpens another." Who better to hold us lovingly accountable than our spouse? This type of critique should never be given in haste or anger. It should only be done in a lovingly honest way. When considering whether you need to confront your spouse, stop and think. You can use the word THINK as an acronym to ask yourself: is what I am about to say True; is it going to be Helpful; can I say it in a way that will Inspire my spouse; is it Necessary; finally, is my approach going to be Kind? Although biblically reproving your spouse may seem intimidating and difficult, if you bring it before God, He will give you the grace you need to accomplish it. Remember, you too are a sinner, so above all, approach your spouse humbly. Not always, but most of the time, when we correct our spouse in the right way, it turns out better than we anticipate and draws us closer together in the process.

Be attentive to the five components of communication—content, tone, body language, timing, and listening—and practice any areas that need refinement. Remember, communication is the lifeblood of a healthy marriage.

COMPLETE THE QUESTIONS ON THE FOLLOWING PAGES

Please answer all of the following questions independently of your fiancé. Do not compare your answers until our next session.

1. Which of the communication styles below describe your fiancé? Mark all that apply.

CHECK ALL THAT APPLY
Communicates with lack of detail
Communicates with excessive detail
Communicates with a loud or angry voice
Fails to communicate things that I should know; for example, does not tell me about an upcoming social engagement until days after they knew about it
Often does not communicate what they are really thinking
Often becomes defensive when discussing things
Communicates intentionally hurtful things
Retreats and stops communicating at all
Other

2. **On a scale of 1 to 10, ten being best, how would you rate your partner's listening skills?**

3. **Does your fiancé interrupt you? If yes, how does it make you feel?**

4. How often does your fiancé criticize you?

5. Give an example of when your fiancé was brutally honest instead of lovingly honest with you. How could they have communicated better in that situation?

6. When you are in the sweet spot in your relationship, do you still experience communication problems?

SESSION FOUR

Chapter 12

RESOLVING CONFLICT

*When a man's ways are pleasing to the LORD,
he makes even his enemies live at peace with him — Proverbs 16:7*

ALTHOUGH COUPLES STRIVE FOR PEACE IN MARRIAGE, THEY ARE destined to have some conflict. Numerous factors contribute to conflict: our sinful nature, sharing physical space, and having ideas, desires, and preferences that collide. Though disagreements are inevitable, conflict should not build walls of resentment or erupt into full-out wars but instead should be opportunities for growth and understanding. Conflict doesn't destroy marriages. However, the inability to resolve conflict does.

Our different personality types and learned behaviors from our family of origin play into how we are conditioned to respond to conflict. Three common unhealthy responses are:

WIN—YOUR GOAL IS TO WIN THE CONFLICT
This is the "I win; you lose" or "I'm right; you're wrong" position. Your spouse's opinion and feelings are second to your need to win. Instead of considering or listening to your partner's point of view, this displays your competitive side, your goal of consistently winning, or your "I know it all" attitude.

WITHDRAW—YOUR GOAL IS TO WITHDRAW FROM CONFLICT
This is the "I don't care" position. You may see no hope in resolution, or you don't want the dispute to escalate. Above all, you want to avoid the discomfort of dealing with the conflict, so you withdraw physically or give your partner the silent treatment in a passive-aggressive way.

YIELD—YOUR GOAL IS TO YIELD TO CONFLICT
This is when you go along with your partner's demands or agree with their position rather than risk a confrontation. Once again, you want to avoid the discomfort of conflict. You would rather stuff your feelings and give in than argue with your partner. You minimize or dismiss your own needs and opinions, not wanting to take a stand against an angry or demanding spouse.

There are problems with all these responses. Instead of encouraging peace in your relationship, these flawed responses promote frustration, resentment, and anger. God wants your marriage to cultivate oneness through committing to work together as a team in every area of life. If one person's personality or preferences are squelched while the other always gets their way, you're not working as a team. To keep a relationship strong, both people need to feel heard. Therefore, your marriage relationship needs to be based on absolute honesty and openness. The goal is not to win, withdraw, or yield but to resolve conflict—sometimes through compromise—with respect and love.

Not all conflicts require major confrontation. This does not mean avoiding conflict; it only means that minor conflicts often resolve themselves easily.

Marcus and Amanda were planning an amazing wedding, but there was one major issue they were unable to resolve. Their parents were giving them a fixed amount for the wedding; however, it would not be enough to cover the extra fifty people Amanda wanted to invite. Marcus did not want to spend all their savings, but Amanda wanted all the important people in her life to be present at their wedding. They were out of solutions, and neither was willing to budge. Like most couples, they had no system to resolve this conflict.

Conflict doesn't destroy marriages:
the inability to resolve conflict does.

Not all conflicts can be resolved quickly—especially when anger, blaming, or defensiveness is present. More significant conflicts or recurring unresolved disputes will eventually bring bitterness and resentment. Unsettled conflicts will fester if ignored.

By using some conflict resolution skills that we will teach in our next session, Marcus and Amanda were able to arrive at a peaceful solution, and the wedding was spectacular. They ended up adding thirty people, Marcus agreed to use some of their savings, and both agreed to work some overtime to make up the savings they were going to spend.

HERE ARE SOME SUGGESTIONS TO CONSIDER WHEN RESOLVING CONFLICT

- Consider a "win-win" position—where you and your partner compromise and come to a solution that benefits both.

- Focus on the present. If you're holding on to old hurts and resentments, your ability to see the reality of the current situation will be impaired. Focus on what you can do in the here-and-now to solve this problem.

- Instead of thinking that your partner needs to change or that you are incompatible, concentrate on the changes that you *can* make. Remember that conflicts are growth opportunities for you and your partner.

- Know when to let something go. If you can't come to an agreement, agree to disagree. Above all, pick your battles. Consider whether the issue is worth disrupting the peace in your relationship.

- Don't always insist on being right or having the final say. If you are right, no defense is needed. If you are wrong, no defense will do.

- When a conflict arises, look for a lesson that God may be teaching you. For example, if you give your partner their way in a decision, God will have done good work in your life by your expression of sacrificial, selfless love (agape).

- Make a promise that no matter how angry you become with your partner, you will never threaten the marriage by speaking of or alluding to divorce.

- Be ready to forgive and forget and move past the conflict without holding resentment or anger. Refer to Chapter 3 for more information on forgiveness.

Remember, conflict does not destroy marriages. It is the inability to resolve conflict that destroys marriages. Disputes can trigger strong emotions that lead to hurt feelings, disappointment, and discomfort. However, when handled in a healthy way, conflict can increase our understanding of one another, build trust, and ultimately strengthen our marriages.

> God's Word challenges us to restore peace. "'In your anger do not sin': Do not let the sun go down while you are still angry" (Ephesians 4:26). It may not be possible to completely resolve an issue before you go to bed at night but have a pact that if you are arguing as bedtime nears, you will acknowledge that you both still love one another, give each other a hug, and agree to resolve the issue later.

When you meet with your mentor couple for this session, they will give you a specific 10-step formula that will help you resolve your major conflicts and restore peace to your relationship.

COMPLETE THE QUESTIONS ON THE FOLLOWING PAGES

Session 4 | Chapter 12 | Resolving Conflict

Please answer the following questions independently of your fiancé. Do not compare your answers until our next session.

1. What is the difference between a discussion and an argument?

2. Name one or more minor conflicts in your relationship that do not need to be resolved (a minor conflict is a disagreement that does not cause harm to the relationship or a conflict that will go away on its own).

3. List one or more moderate conflicts in your relationship (a moderate conflict is a conflict that does not threaten a healthy relationship, but its resolution would generate more harmony).

4. List one or more major conflicts in your relationship (a major conflict is a significant issue that, if left unresolved, would damage or threaten a healthy relationship; or a recurring dispute that continually causes dissension).

Please go to www.marriagebygod.org and watch the Conflict Resolution Video *under the resources tab, as part of your homework assignment. This is something you can do together or on your own.*

 CONGRATULATIONS! YOU'VE FINISHED SESSION FOUR

NOTES

SESSION FIVE

Chapter 13

EMOTIONAL INTIMACY

Two are better than one — Ecclesiastes 4:9

THERE IS AN EXHILARATION AND ENERGY TO NEW, ROMANTIC LOVE. AS a couple explores getting to know one another, they find themselves thrilled to talk about anything and everything. They are curious and delighted to learn as much as possible about each other. As the relationship grows, they begin to share more deeply their dreams and goals for the future.

Fast forward several years, and it is not uncommon to see this same couple experiencing an emotional distance in their relationship. They live and sleep together every day but are more like roommates than the two people who were once so close. How does this happen? Where did the emotional intimacy go that once drew them so close?

> *Intimacy* often refers to a physical or sexual relationship. However, *emotional intimacy* and *sexual intimacy* are not synonymous. Emotional intimacy is about being comfortable and safe enough to share your innermost thoughts and feelings. It is about expressing your fears, hopes, and dreams without facing judgment. Perhaps the best way to define emotional intimacy is to think of the phrase "into-me-see."

A marriage relationship should provide a safe place for a couple to know and be known on more than a superficial level. It is a secure bond where partners can readily share their struggles and concerns, as well as their joys and successes. A husband and wife should lovingly discuss their big decisions and decide them together. The emotional intimacy afforded in marriage should provide both partners with a secure environment for sharing vulnerably while our partner listens with understanding and empathy.

This chapter will examine the necessary elements for experiencing emotional intimacy. We will also look at some common roadblocks that hinder closeness and growth in a relationship. Finally, you'll evaluate the level of emotional intimacy in your relationship.

God created us in His image, including being made with some of the same relational characteristics as the Triune God. We have the capacity and desire for connection, closeness, community, and dependency. God planned for married couples to meet many of each other's needs for love and connection through the oneness of marriage. Emotional intimacy cultivates oneness. Satan's number one attack on marriages is to destroy the oneness in marriage.

Some of the most essential elements of emotional intimacy are unconditional (agape) love, commitment, trust, respect, honesty, and vulnerability. Emotional intimacy exists when two people are committed to the well-being and development of each other, fully trust each other, and know they are perfectly safe with each other.

Fear is one of the biggest deterrents to emotional intimacy. Fear can come in many forms: the fear of trusting, rejection, judgment, losing control, appearing weak, or getting a negative response. God does not want us to fear emotional intimacy in our marriage for any reason. This type of fear is not from God. "There is no fear in love. But perfect love drives out fear because fear has to do with punishment. The one who fears is not made perfect in love" (1 John 4:18). We have not counted for ourselves but have been told there are 365 times the Bible says, "fear not." That is one for every day of the year. God doesn't want us to go a single day without embracing these words of comfort.

Fear is one of the biggest deterrents to emotional intimacy.

Sometimes hurts and traumas from our past cause fear or make it hard for us to trust others. If this is true, you can improve your relationship by healing those wounds. Relationship experts and marriage counselors Milan and Kay Yerkovich have devoted much of their life's work helping couples understand how early life experiences can impede their ability to love correctly and thus affect their intimacy:

> *Many people who lacked deep emotional connection as children resist looking back, some of them even go to the point of denying that the past is significant. Yet, in many cases, the stronger the resistance to looking back, the greater that need actually is … the entire point of our work: to put the past in the past so we can get on with our present lives. But the simple fact is that before we can learn how to love correctly, we need to see clearly how the past has shaped us.*[8]

This imprint from our family of origin shapes our behaviors, beliefs, and expectations of all relationships, especially our marriages. Consider how your early experiences of care and comfort (or lack of care and comfort)—especially from your parents—have shaped your ability and desire for connection and closeness.

---

[8] Milan and Kay Yerkovich, *How We Love: Discover Your Love Style, Enhance Your Marriage* (Colorado: Waterbrook, 2011), pg 24.

ROADBLOCKS TO EMOTIONAL INTIMACY

Numerous behaviors and responses can be roadblocks to emotional intimacy in marriage. Here are some of the most common:

1. INDEPENDENCE

Being independent is when a husband or wife tends to be private, is unwilling to share thoughts and feelings, appears self-sufficient, prefers taking care of his or her own needs, and does not involve a spouse in decision-making. As you enter marriage, you should strive for neither independence nor overdependence but rather for healthy interdependence.

2. AVOIDANCE

Being avoidant is when a husband or wife withdraws when upset, prefers not to deal with conflict, and perhaps becomes angry if his or her spouse expresses emotions or needs. Placating is a form of being avoidant: attempting to avoid conflict or hostility by making concessions or appeasing. As a result, the other spouse often feels emotionally detached from the avoidant spouse.

3. PASSIVE-AGGRESSIVENESS

Being passive-aggressive is when a husband or wife prefers to be passive (silent) rather than express honest feelings or directly confront issues, but then acts out in negative ways. Passive-aggressive people don't always exhibit outward anger or appear malicious—instead, they may procrastinate, blame, sulk, be chronically late, and resist accomplishing requested or expected tasks.

4. SARCASM

Being sarcastic is when a husband or wife jokes around using irony to mock or convey their dissatisfaction. Sarcasm is criticism and is often accompanied by negative attitudes such as disapproval, contempt, scorn, and ridicule. Sarcasm in marriage can be annoying, hurtful, and destructive.

The behaviors detailed above are detrimental to growing intimacy in marriage. Other damaging behaviors to oneness include self-pity, non-biblical criticism, defensiveness, the inability to listen to another's point of view and take correction, and excessive anger. All of these behaviors are sinful.

If the emotional intimacy you desire with your fiancé needs improvement, start by looking at your own actions and behaviors. Sin is one of the biggest obstacles that blocks emotional intimacy. Get quiet before God and ask Him to reveal any sin in your life that may be disrupting your closeness. Vulnerability with your fiancé begins with vulnerability with God. We can only truly embrace the "two hearts becoming one" relationship by placing God at the center of our relationship and fully submitting to Him. If you are struggling with sin, confess it to God and repent. Then humbly share your struggle with your future spouse in a transparent, honest conversation. The discussion questions at the end of this chapter will help get you started.

Emotional intimacy does not mean you will see everything eye-to-eye with your fiancé. Instead, it means that when you disagree (which should happen in a healthy relationship), you can still be sensitive to your partner's point of view. Emotional intimacy gives you the confidence to discuss differences within a safe environment and to compromise together when necessary.

Vulnerability with your fiancé begins with vulnerability with God.

Emotional intimacy is something that doesn't just happen. As you come together in marriage, if you are not careful, you will find yourselves reacting to all that life throws your way with little time left over for investing emotionally into your relationship. Emotional intimacy requires an intentional effort to keep it alive and growing in marriage. To continue developing a deeper knowledge and understanding ("into-me-see") between you and your future spouse, you need to continue to plan intentional special time together. Continue dating one another after you marry. Ask each other meaningful, fun, and creative questions that allow you to share your hearts. If you can't think of things to discuss, there is a resource provided on our website at https://marriagebygod.com/couple-conversation-starters/.

Don't forget: the more emotionally intimate you are with your future spouse, the more likely you both will reach out to meet each other's needs. May this be the kind of intimacy that you experience in your marriage!

COMPLETE THE QUESTIONS ON THE FOLLOWING PAGES

*Please answer the following questions independently of your fiancé.
Do not compare your answers until our next session.*

1. On a scale of 1 to 10 (10 being best), rate the accuracy of the following statements.

STATEMENT	RATING
I feel emotionally connected and understood by my fiancé.	
I feel comfortable and safe sharing my deepest thoughts and feelings with my fiancé.	
I trust my fiancé to keep my confidences.	
I feel my fiancé knows me better than any other person.	
I believe we will make important decisions together as a team in marriage.	
In marriage, I believe we will hold each other accountable in a God-honoring way.	
We pray together as a couple on a regular basis.	

2. What is the biggest deterrent to being more vulnerable with your fiancé (such as fear of trusting, rejection, judgment, losing control, appearing weak, or getting a negative response)?

3. Do you see any negative behaviors hindering emotional intimacy in your relationship (such as avoidance, sarcasm, passive-aggressive behavior, criticism, nagging, anger, self-pity, defensiveness, or family-of-origin imprints)?

4. Technology plays an important role in our lives. Are there any changes you would like to make in your relationship regarding the use of technology that could improve your connectedness as a couple?

5. Complete this statement, "This is what I would like you to know about me in order to understand me better …"

SESSION FIVE

Chapter 14

PHYSICAL INTIMACY

I am my lover's and my lover is mine
— Song of Songs 6:3

WHEN GOD FIRST PLACED ADAM AND EVE IN THE GARDEN, THEY WERE fully connected in physical and emotional oneness. Genesis 2:25 says, "The man and his wife were both naked, and they felt no shame." In his book, *A Celebration of Sex*, Dr. Douglas Rosenau comments insightfully on this passage:

> *It is tremendously moving to think of God's original one-flesh companionship. Adam and Eve, before the fall of Eden, had the marvelous capacity of being totally naked, physically and emotionally, with no shame or fear. They reveled in a childlike trust and curiosity— laughing, exploring, giving and receiving love. Sex was a glorious, innocent celebration lived out with instinctual honesty, respect, and zest for life. It was naked and unashamed with no performance anxiety, inhibitions, pain, or selfish skill deficits. What a relationship and sex life they were able to have as they truly "knew" each other, inside and out!* [9]

Unlike any other relationship, God gives a husband and wife the sexual union as an exclusive way to express their love for one another. The Song of Solomon is a beautiful, descriptive book found in the Old Testament that narrates the sensuous coming together of a husband and wife in eros love. We understand what God thinks about sex through the Song of Solomon—and it is good!

God has ordained that sexual intimacy should only take place in the framework of marriage. Sadly, Satan often takes God's goodness and distorts it. Many today see God's rules in this area as archaic and condemning. But God has placed these commands in place for our protection. He wants to protect us from the heartache of infidelity and broken relationships. When a couple chooses to have premarital sex, they have opened the door to having sex outside of marriage. If a couple does this before marriage, it weakens their resolve to stay faithful within the marriage (especially when things are not going well). Conversely, when a couple chooses to discipline themselves in this way before marriage, it shows their commitment to being faithful within their marriage.

---

[9] Douglas E. Rosenau, *A Celebration of Sex* (Tennessee: Thomas Nelson, 2002), pg 4.

If you have been faithful to follow God's perfect plan for your relationship and have remained sexually pure, then you will receive God's fullest blessing. If you have succumbed to the temptation of premarital sex, we want to challenge you to turn away from this choice and commit to doing it God's way until your wedding night. We serve an amazing God of forgiveness who gives us second chances. If you desire to begin doing things God's way, start by genuinely repenting before God and committing to turn away from sexual sin. "If we confess our sins, He is faithful and just and will forgive us our sins and purify us from all unrighteousness" (1 John 1:9). In essence, you become a reborn virgin.

Different from any other relationship,
God gives a husband and wife the sexual union as an exclusive way
to express their love for one another.

There still may be ramifications to the choices you have made, but God will walk beside you as you deal with any of the consequences. One such repercussion could be struggling to forgive either yourself or your future spouse for the past. God has forgiven you; it is essential to forgive yourself and release any guilt you may be experiencing. Romans 8:1 tells us, "Therefore, there is now no condemnation for those who are in Christ Jesus." Additionally, just as you are forgiven, you also need to forgive your partner for their past. Then you can enter your marriage with God's fullest blessing.

If you are a virgin (or a reborn virgin), you have a beautiful gift to give to your spouse on your wedding night. It will show your fiancé your commitment to staying faithful once you are married.

> God uses the physical intimacy between a husband and wife to do far more than just satisfy a physical need and express marital love. Sexual love also communicates commitment, caring, understanding, fun, forgiveness, and intimate friendship. It is one of the most intense ways a husband and wife express their exclusive oneness. A vital element for having a vibrant sex life is communicating openly and honestly. Below are some things to consider and perhaps discuss.

THE BIOLOGY IS DIFFERENT BETWEEN MEN AND WOMEN

When it comes to sex, family therapist Gary Smalley describes men as microwave ovens and women as Crock-Pots®. Most men can achieve an orgasm in just a few minutes of focused concentration and stimulation. However, it usually requires an average of ten to thirty minutes of focused concentration and appropriate stimulation for a woman to reach a sexual climax. Due to these differences, you will want to understand your spouse's needs. Additionally, it is not necessary that both partners always reach an orgasm to have a satisfying sexual experience. Because of the additional energy and focus needed for a woman to climax, it might be more gratifying for her to just share physical and emotional closeness with her husband on a particularly stress-filled day.

Husbands typically have higher sex drives than their wives. There is a legitimate biological reason that a man needs more regular sex. A husband is physically satisfied right after sexual intimacy. Then as sperm begins to build again in his testicles, the physical need intensifies for a man to experience sexual release. As this happens, he has more sexual thoughts and is more easily aroused. Just as your body tells you when you are hungry, thirsty, or tired, a man's body also tells him when he needs sexual release.

> *God uses the physical intimacy between a husband and wife to communicate love, commitment, caring understanding, fun, forgiveness, and intimate friendship.*

BE HONEST WITH YOUR SPOUSE ABOUT YOUR SEXUAL NEEDS AND WANTS

Mutually satisfying sexual intimacy requires being both selfish and unselfish. Great lovers know their bodies and enjoy their sexual feelings, as well as know and meet their partner's sexual needs. Ask your spouse what would make sexual intimacy more pleasurable for them and share what is pleasing to you. Remember, your spouse cannot read your mind. Sharing your needs and wants will not take the romance out of your sexual experience. On the contrary, it allows for better sexual intimacy. Your spouse will gain more enjoyment if they know that you are enjoying the experience, too. The goal should be to combine the best of what you both desire to celebrate a rich sex life together.

MEN AND WOMEN HAVE DIFFERENT EMOTIONAL AND SEXUAL DESIRES AND NEEDS

Although a husband and wife are meant to meet each other's emotional and physical intimacy needs, God created them with different needs and responses. In general, a woman needs to feel a sense of emotional intimacy with her husband to desire him sexually. If a wife is experiencing tension with her husband or is physically exhausted, making love will likely be the last thing on her mind. Conversely, a man will be drawn into a more powerful emotional intimacy with his wife through sex. A man will likely still be sexually attracted to his wife and desire sexual intimacy even if there is tension in the marriage. If he feels exhausted, he probably won't want to invest in emotional intimacy, but he may enjoy engaging in lovemaking as a release from tension and exhaustion. Remember, he has an actual physical need for sexual release. A wife should be sensitive to meeting her husband's physical needs. The good news is that a man who has his physical needs met by his wife is usually more engaged in meeting her emotional needs.

HUSBANDS SHOULD INVEST IN CREATING AN EMOTIONAL ONENESS WITH THEIR WIVES AS THE FIRST STEP IN FOREPLAY

Consider setting the environment early in the day through a loving note, calling from work to say, "I love you," listening to her and connecting with her emotionally, relieving her of some of the demands of her daily chores, or providing time for her to unwind with a bubble bath. A husband will honor God by being a student of his wife, developing a greater capacity for emotional intimacy, and giving special attention to the environment that will light her fire.

USE YOUR FIVE SENSES—SIGHT, TOUCH, SOUND, SMELL, AND TASTE

God has designed our sexual relationship with our spouse to be enjoyed through our senses. So, be creative and invest time in finding ways to use your senses to create an exciting sex life. Here are a few ideas:

SIGHT

Create soft lighting. Because men tend to be visually stimulated, you should consider choosing lingerie that your husband will enjoy. Have fun disrobing in front of him. It is pleasing to your husband to view you naked.

TOUCH

Make sure the room is at a suitable temperature. A gentle massage can be an excellent way to get things started. Pay attention to neglected areas like ears, neck, inner thighs, etc. Use massage oil, or softly tickle with a feather. Use your imagination…

SOUND

Music can be a sensual way to set the mood. So, keep a playlist with your favorite romantic tunes at hand.

SMELL

Odors can make or break a sexual encounter. Be sure to practice good hygiene. Put on your spouse's favorite perfume or cologne. Create a wonderful aroma through candles.

TASTE

Like smell, taste can be memorable. Be sure you have fresh breath. Sip your favorite beverage. Have some of your favorite flavorful treats to lead into a romantic evening.

The five senses can create an amorous environment, but they can also kill the mood: the television blaring, bright lighting, the possibility of being interrupted by children, or time constraints will not be the environment conducive for most (especially women) to fully enjoy a romantic encounter. Use your imagination with all your five senses and keep your sexually intimate times full of fun and variety.

SELF-ACCEPTANCE, SELF-ESTEEM, AND A GOOD BODY IMAGE ARE VITALLY IMPORTANT

There has never been anyone else God created who is just like you. He designed us to have individual gifts, talents, and abilities, and we need to embrace our physical differences. As Christians, we should honor God by having a good self-image—accepting ourselves without comparing ourselves to others. No matter how beautiful others may tell a woman she is, she still tends to feel insecure about her looks. Remember, your spouse was attracted to you above anyone else. As a husband, strengthen how your wife feels about herself by telling her you find her attractive.

Pay attention to your health, maintain good hygiene, and incorporate regular exercise into your life to help your body image. Take care of the body that God gave you. Equally important is to accept the natural changes that occur through life such as, pregnancy, health conditions, and aging.

KEEP YOUR SPOUSE'S SEXUAL NEEDS A PRIORITY

The sex drive between husbands and wives is rarely equal. There will be times when one spouse (usually the husband) will be more interested in sex than the other. Agape love involves selflessness. Look to meet your spouse's sexual needs even if you are not in the mood because it is the loving thing to do.

A wise wife will not ignore her husband's sexual needs. Instead, she will offer her body as a gift, not using excuses such as being too tired, too busy, or having a headache. (In fact, studies have shown that sexual activity can be the best medicine to get rid of a headache.) She may, at times, meet her husband's needs through brief encounters (quickies) to satisfy his need for release. However, he should also be sensitive to making sure that they slow things down for a more mutually pleasing encounter at other times. And sometimes the couple may want to make a special occasion of the event.

Another significant detail that plays into a couple's sexual fulfillment is the rise and fall of testosterone during a woman's monthly menstrual cycle. This varies significantly throughout the month and will affect her sexual desire and enjoyment. Below are some fun facts shared by Gabrielle Lichterman, author and founder of Hormonology at www.myhormonology.com. They identify the specific days of a women's menstrual cycle when sex will be most enjoyable. A husband and wife might benefit from paying attention to this monthly cycle.

THE HORMONOLOGY GUIDE TO SEX

- **RED HOT DAYS :** Day 1 (first day of menstruation) to Day 14 (ovulation), peaking on Day 13 and remaining high on Day 14.

- **LUKEWARM DAYS :** Day 15 to Day 23

- **BONUS RED HOT DAYS :** Day 24 to the end of her cycle.

- **ULTIMATE TIME FOR SEX :** The morning of Day 13. "The morning is when a man's testosterone peaks in his 24-hour hormone cycle. And Day 13 is when testosterone peaks in a woman's monthly hormone cycle. When these two hormonal peaks intersect, they can set the stage for the best sex all month long," states Lichterman.[10] Mark your calendars!

Physical intimacy should be a celebration of your one-flesh companionship. Husbands and wives should come together with a childlike trust and curiosity—laughing, exploring, and giving and receiving love. Keep your romance alive and your physical intimacy vibrant. Neglecting this area of your marriage deprives you and your spouse of the extraordinary union that God created for you.

COMPLETE THE QUESTIONS ON THE FOLLOWING PAGE

---

[10] Armen Hareyan, "Women Can Now Predict When They Will Have The Best Sex," *EmaxHealth*, posted January 20, 2006, accessed June 25 2012, http://www.emaxhealth.com/48/4247.html.

Session 5 | Chapter 14 | Physical Intimacy

Please answer the following questions independently of your fiancé. Do not compare your answers until our next session.

1. Are you comfortable discussing your future sexual needs in marriage with your fiancé?

2. What concerns or fears do you have concerning sex?

3. What issue or experience from your or your partner's past may affect your intimacy?

4. How many times per week do you think you will desire sex in marriage? Your spouse-to-be?

5. What are some creative ways you can keep the romance in your relationship?

SESSION FIVE

Chapter 15

AFFAIR-PROOFING YOUR MARRIAGE

Marriage should be honored by all, and the marriage bed kept pure, for God will judge the adulterer and all the sexually immoral — Hebrews 13:4

"I COULD NEVER HAVE AN AFFAIR! AFFAIRS ONLY HAPPEN TO OTHER couples." If that is how you feel, then the first thing you need to recognize is that *no one* is immune to an affair. The truth is that most couples that have experienced an extramarital affair are caught off guard. They never planned to have an affair.

In the general population, some reports suggest an astounding 50 to 60 percent of husbands and an equally shocking 45 to 55 percent of wives have had an affair by the time they are forty.[11] The incidence of infidelity between Christians is probably close to that of the general population.[12] An additional study of pastors sponsored by *Christianity Today* found that 23 percent of the 300 pastors surveyed admitted to sexually inappropriate behavior with someone other than their wives while in the ministry.[13] People are often shocked at how unexpectedly they fall victim to sexually inappropriate behavior.

Cody was a young, devoted Christian man, committed to staying sexually pure until marriage. However, he had one secret he was not proud of that he kept from his fiancé. A family member had exposed him to pornography at a young age, and he had continued regular viewing. Although it made him feel dirty, he justified to himself that it was helping him stay pure until their wedding night. He would stop as soon as they were married. Soon after they married, Cody realized that although he was extremely attracted to his beautiful young bride, he was addicted to pornography. Katy was devastated when she found Cody viewing pornography late one evening.

Cody was immediately remorseful and admitted he needed help. Katy knew she needed to forgive Cody, but it would be a complex process to work through. The trust in their relationship had to be rebuilt as well. He had been so secretive about this; she wondered if there were other things he was hiding from her.

---

[11] Grant L. Martin. "Relationship, Romance, and Sexual Addiction in Extramarital Affairs," *Journal of Psychology and Christianity* 8, no. 4, (Winter 1989): pg 5.

[12] Dave Carder, *Torn Asunder: Recovering from an Extramarital Affair* (Chicago: Moody, 2008), pg 25.

[13] D.J.P. Hudson. "Predictors of Infidelity among Pastors," (masters's thesis, Biola University, 1998).

Cody took action and sought the proper help he needed to break his addiction. As part of his restorative process, he put safeguards on all his devices and asked a trusted Christian mentor to be his accountability partner. Following God's example, in time, Katy fully forgave Cody; Cody was able to forgive himself, and trust was rebuilt in their relationship. Although they never would have wished this upon anyone, they were able to see how, in the end, this painful experience drew them closer together when they sought to heal God's way.

> God is clear that the marital bed should be kept pure (Hebrews 13:4). Sexual sin includes not only physical adultery but also lusting. Jesus said, "You have heard that it was said, 'Do not commit adultery.' But I tell you that anyone who looks at a woman lustfully has already committed adultery with her in his heart" (Matthew 5:27–28). The *Merriam-Webster Dictionary* defines lust as "an intense longing or craving." A quick, passing thought about someone being attractive is not a sin, but an excessive craving or lusting after someone is akin to committing adultery in the eyes of God.

Protecting your relationship involves establishing boundaries that should be defined, implemented, and respected at all times. Just as you cannot inoculate against the flu once you come down with it, so you cannot protect against an affair after it has happened.

Randy and Ashley had known each other since they were neighbors in grade school. He was like a big brother to this little tomboy who was two years younger than he. They grew up as the best of buddies. Shortly after Randy achieved his dream of becoming a firefighter, he announced that he was marrying his long-time girlfriend, Jessica. Ashley was so happy for him.

After they got married, Randy and Jessica would often double date with Ashley and her boyfriend, Josh. Randy had a brotherlike pride when Ashley became a nurse. Since they were in related fields, they would sometimes meet up for lunch when their days off matched up.

As Randy and Jessica decided to start a family, they had difficulty conceiving. Ashley used her medical resources to help them navigate their infertility struggles. Because Ashley knew their circumstances so well, Randy would often vent to her about the extra stress this situation was putting on his relationship with Jessica. Ashley was always understanding and compassionate. Then one day, when they met for lunch, it was Ashley's turn to be consoled. Josh had broken up with her. After a tearful lunch, they decided to go back to her apartment, where they could talk more privately. Ashley sobbed, "Why can't I find someone like you! You are the perfect guy." Randy, who in recent months had been feeling more of an emotional connection with Ashley, embraced her in a heartfelt hug. He told her she deserved to find someone who appreciated all of her wonderful qualities like he did. That day, neither planned to be sexually intimate, but it just moved in that direction.

In the beginning, there had been no threat because their relationship was just a friendship. They didn't think they needed to abide by any archaic boundaries. They never thought something like this could happen to them, but over time, their feelings changed. Since the proper boundaries were never in place, they were unprepared for where things led when feelings changed.

PROTECTING YOUR MARRIAGE

We strongly recommend the following ten protections for your marriage to guard against becoming vulnerable to an affair:

1. KEEP CHRIST AT THE CENTER OF YOUR MARRIAGE
This includes attending church together, reading the Bible together, and most importantly, praying together.

2. FULFILL YOUR SPOUSE'S EMOTIONAL AND PHYSICAL NEEDS
Understand your spouse's needs and seek to meet them. Additionally, understand your own needs and communicate them.

3. SPEND AS MUCH TIME TOGETHER AS POSSIBLE
Intentionally set a tone at home that makes it a place you and your spouse enjoy. Find fun activities to share—plan regular date nights. Your marriage should be based on a solid friendship where you enjoy being together.

4. DO NOT SPEND TOO MUCH TIME WITH ONE COUPLE
When couples spend a lot of time with one another, they invest considerable emotional energy. They hold an important place in each other's lives. It is easy for lines to get blurred. It is not uncommon for them to begin sharing more personally with one another. The familiarity makes it easy for a husband or wife to reach out to the other spouse of the opposite gender for advice or understanding. When you allow a friend of the opposite gender to become more than they should, it is damaging to your marriage. Above all, respect your marriage and be careful to keep good boundaries with other couples. An emotional affair can be as devastating as a physical affair.

5. DO NOT SHARE YOUR MARITAL PROBLEMS WITH ANYONE OF THE OPPOSITE SEX
A husband should not discuss his marital problems with another woman, and a wife should not discuss her marital problems with another man. Decide in advance never to engage in this type of conversation. Do not let anyone of the opposite sex discuss personal issues with you, either.

6. STAY AWAY FROM SINGLES ENVIRONMENTS
Problems can occur when you do activities with single friends that involve them seeking to meet new people of the opposite sex. The different lifestyles between singles and married couples are typically not compatible. Always be with others who encourage your marriage commitment.

7. SAVE ALL YOUR PHYSICAL AFFECTION FOR YOUR SPOUSE
For instance, kissing on the lips and intimate hugs should be reserved for your spouse. If you don't know the difference between a friendly hug and an intimate hug, ask your spouse.

8. GUARD YOUR HEART AND YOUR MIND
Internet connections can start innocently, but they pose the same threat to relationships as in-person encounters. Be sure to honor the exact limits online as you do in person. Set

boundaries with any social networking accounts, and always provide your spouse complete access to your computer and phone. Be alert to any people or opportunities that may tempt your mind to have lustful thoughts. The Internet gives immediate access to pornography. Try to go to bed together to avoid late-night Internet temptations. If you are tempted to view these resources, seek out the accountability of a mature Christian friend. Put software on your computer and devices that will block inappropriate sites. Get the help of a professional, if needed.

9. AVOID SIGNIFICANT FRIENDSHIPS WITH SOMEONE FROM THE OPPOSITE SEX

Couples often enter marriage with a close friend of the opposite sex. Once married, meeting or communicating with this friend alone is no longer appropriate. The workplace can also present situations where you work closely with a coworker of the opposite sex. Be sure to keep the conversation appropriate, avoid social interaction outside of work, and guard your heart. If your spouse is uncomfortable with a relationship you have with anyone of the opposite sex, respect your spouse's feelings and discontinue it no matter how difficult. Your spouse should be more important than any relationship outside your marriage.

10. REALIZE THAT YOUR MARRIAGE IS NOT IMMUNE TO AN AFFAIR

Never let your guard down. Affairs happen to people who least expect it. Set boundaries to protect your marriage and observe them with conviction.

Keeping the home fires warm is one of the best ways to protect your marriage. A marriage is most vulnerable to a spouse seeking validation outside of the marriage when things get cold at home. Remember, you play a big part in your spouse's self-esteem and consequently how they think about the marriage. Be sure to admire and cherish one another and operate as a united team. When love is felt at home, there is no need to look for it elsewhere.

COMPLETE THE QUESTIONS ON THE FOLLOWING PAGES

*Please answer the following questions independently of your fiancé.
Do not compare your answers until our next session.*

1. In which of the following ways do you engage with friends or work associates of the opposite gender, one-to-one, without the knowledge of your fiancé?

   CHECK ALL THAT APPLY
   - Phone calls
   - Email
   - Texting
   - Commenting on social media
   - Private messaging through social media
   - Coffee breaks
   - Meals/drinks together
   - Business meetings
   - Social events

2. Is there any relationship that you can identify as needing additional boundaries? What action steps would you suggest putting into place to improve your hedges?

3. What is your attitude towards pornography?

4. Will you agree to give total access to each other's technology activities?

5. Are you comfortable with the amount of time your fiancé spends away from you? Explain.

6. List five activities or hobbies you enjoy doing together.

 CONGRATULATIONS! YOU'VE FINISHED SESSION FIVE

SESSION SIX

Chapter 16

FINANCES

*No servant can serve two masters. Either he will hate the one and love the other, or he will be devoted to the one and despise the other.
You cannot serve God and Money — Luke 16:13*

JOHN WALKED AT THE BEACH WITH HIS WIFE, CARRIE, THINKING THE relaxed setting would make discussing finances easier. When they saw a man with dirty hair and ragged clothes drinking from something hidden in a brown paper bag, John said to Carrie, "You see that guy there? He is worth $50,000 more than we are." Shocked, Carrie said, "What's he doing homeless?" John explained, "He's a drunk worth nothing, but we're $50,000 in debt."

Many couples today are in debt. It's one of the most prevalent problems in marriages. Couples often argue about money. It is one of the leading causes of divorce. Our schools teach many subjects, but seldom offer classes in money management. Yet not knowing calculus or French won't threaten your marriage, as will poor money management.

The Bible says much about financial management. In fact, money is the second most common theme found in the Bible—only the Kingdom of God is mentioned more. So, as we begin this session on financial principles, let's dispel three common money myths.

MONEY MYTHS

MYTH 1: MONEY IS THE ROOT OF ALL EVIL

In the Bible, it is not money that is evil, but how we regard money: "For the love of money is a root of all kinds of evil" (1 Timothy 6:10). Focusing on money leads to greed, selfish ambition, and pride. Jesus said, "No servant can serve two masters. Either he will hate the one and love the other, or he will be devoted to the one and despise the other. You cannot serve both God and Money" (Luke 16:13).

MYTH 2: IT IS A SIN TO BE RICH

The Bible does not say it is a sin to be rich. Many prominent and righteous people in the Bible were among the wealthiest people of their day: Abraham, Joseph, Job, King David, and King Solomon. In reality, "The earth is the LORD'S and everything in it" (Psalm 24:1). We are merely stewards of God's possessions.

MYTH 3: IT IS A SIN TO BE POOR

Some believe that if they have enough faith, God will bless them with financial riches along with anything else they desire. Some call this the name-it-and-claim-it theology. They believe that a lack of wealth is the result of a lack of faith. Or they may judge those who lack wealth as lacking God's favor. The truth is that God does not promise wealth and riches to those who are faithful. God does, however, promise to meet our *needs*: "And my God will meet all your needs according to His glorious riches in Christ Jesus" (Philippians 4:19).

Studies show that the average American family will spend over 80 percent of their income repaying debt.

The United States leads the world in areas, especially finances, yet the average American saves less than individuals in many other industrial countries. According to *Expert Market*, Americans save on average 4.97% of their household income. Below is how that compares to the top five countries.[14]

COUNTRY	SAVINGS
Switzerland	19.3%
Sweden	15.72%
Norway	9.11%
Australia	9.23%
Germany	9.52%

Most Americans would be unable to survive financially if they had to go without income for six months. This lack of savings carries adverse consequences. For example, when emergencies arise (and they will), a low or nonexistent savings cushion stresses and strains both the budget and the marriage. Couples may be forced to borrow money, incurring debt payments and interest fees.

MOST COUPLES HAVE FINANCIAL PROBLEMS FOR ONE OF THESE REASONS

LACK OF FINANCIAL PLANNING OR ORGANIZATION

The proverb, "Failing to plan is planning to fail," is often attributed to author Alan Lakein. We tend to be emotional about money. When emotions are high, it's easy to make fiscal mistakes.

---

[14] "These Are the Countries That Save the Most Money Around the World," *Expert Market*, accessed October 25, 2021, https://www.expertmarket.com/credit-card-processing/countries-that-save-the-most-money.

However, if we develop a plan when not emotionally stressed, we are more likely to work together towards our goals. A free online resource that can assist you with watching your expenses and evaluating your financial goals is www.mint.com.

LACK OF FINANCIAL KNOWLEDGE

We should be lifelong students of economic principles. It is crucial that both husband and wife stay informed about the family's finances.

LACK OF FINANCIAL INDEPENDENCE

When we become adults, we usually become financially responsible for ourselves. This transition is not always easy, and sometimes there are setbacks. If you and your spouse find yourselves dependent on others—perhaps due to unforeseen circumstances—strive for financial independence. Don't rely on a future inheritance, which is another form of financial dependence, for circumstances can change, and the inheritance might not come or might be less than expected. We should always practice good stewardship by living within our means at our current income.

LACK OF FACING OUR FINANCIAL REALITY

We might be telling ourselves that we will begin to manage our money wisely after we make "just one last purchase." This is like thinking that we will start a diet tomorrow after one more splurge on a one-pound box of chocolate today! Sometimes people procrastinate practicing good money management because they would rather be in denial about their financial situation. Unfortunately, one more purchase digs the debt hole that much deeper.

LACK OF FINANCIAL CONTENTMENT

No matter how much we have, it's easy to want just a little more. The Apostle Paul wrote, "I know what it is to be in need, and I know what it is to have plenty. I have learned the secret of being content in any and every situation, whether well fed or hungry, whether living in plenty or in want" (Philippians 4:12). God promises to meet our needs, not necessarily all that we want. "And my God will supply every need of yours according to His riches in glory in Christ Jesus" (Philippians 4:19). We should practice having an attitude of gratitude and focusing on being appreciative to God for what we have.

LACK OF ABILITY TO DELAY GRATIFICATION

More than ever, we live in an instant gratification generation—fast food, video on demand, instantaneous pain relief, and buy now, pay later. We want what we want, and we want it NOW. The ability to make immediate credit card purchases enables easy debt. We need to discipline ourselves with our finances.

Many believe financial security is based on how much income we make in our careers. That's only one factor among several: how much you make, how much you spend, and how wisely you save and invest. You cannot always control how much you earn. You can, however, limit how much you spend, determine how much you will save, and plan for how much you will invest.

Session 6 | Chapter 16 | Finances

CONSIDER HOW TWO COUPLES' DECISIONS AFFECTED THEIR FINANCIAL SECURITY AND FUTURE

TREVOR AND JULIE

Trevor and Julie were both public school teachers. They had three children. Trevor worked summer school every year to earned extra income. Except for their house and cars, they bought nothing they couldn't afford to pay for at the time of purchase and thus avoided paying high-interest rates. They paid their credit cards in full every month. They bought used cars and drove them for at least seven years. By careful planning, they were able to take a nice vacation every year with their kids (in later years, even traveling to Australia). When interest rates went down, they refinanced their house into a fifteen-year loan. By the time they retired at age sixty-five, they owned their home free and clear, both cars were paid off, and all three kids had graduated from state colleges. They looked forward to a comfortable retirement.

CLIFF AND ANDREA

Cliff and Andrea both made substantial incomes in sales jobs, often receiving large bonus checks. They had one daughter, Sarah. Because of their demanding jobs, they frequently ate out, had a gardener and a housekeeper, took their cars to the car wash weekly, and had most of their clothes dry-cleaned. They believed that since they were in sales, appearance was important. They wanted to show how successful they were, so they leased a new Lexus every three years. Every year they enjoyed both an exotic tropical vacation and a cruise. As their home appreciated, they refinanced and took money out to augment their lifestyle. When the economy plunged, so did their incomes. They continued to spend at the same level by using credit, expecting the economy to improve soon. Modifying the spending habits they had developed in more prosperous times proved difficult. By the time Sarah was ready for college, they were heavily in debt with no equity in their home. Although they had always promised to pay for Sarah to attend a four-year private university, their only option was for her to live at home while attending community college. Later, Sarah took out student loans to finish two years at a local state college. Because they had very little savings, Cliff and Andrea had to withdraw retirement funds to pay some emergency medical bills, incurring tax penalties on their retirement account. They reached 65 knowing they would need to postpone retirement for many years.

Cliff and Andrea made substantially more money over the years than Trevor and Julie. Yet Trevor and Julie managed their money responsibly. They made conservative, careful choices in how they spent, saved, and invested their money, living in ways that encouraged a secure financial future.

A FEW TIPS TO HELP YOU WITH YOUR PLANNING

- Borrowing is not a sin, but bondage to debt is. It makes you a slave to the lender. "Let no debt remain outstanding, except the continuing debt to love one another" (Romans 13:8).

- The average credit card debt of U.S. families is $6,270,[15] according to the most recent data from the Federal Reserve's Survey of Consumer Finances. As a result, many of us need plastic surgery: we need to cut up the cards that enable us to acquire debt.

- Your bank ledger reveals your financial values. See if your ledger reflects the values you wish to display.

- Before you make a purchase, ask yourself three questions: (1) Do I really need it? (2) Can I afford it? (3) Is it worth it?

Your bank ledger reveals your financial values.

- Any time you spend money, visualize the purchase in one-dollar bills. Unfortunately, credit cards, debit cards, Apple Pay, etc., make spending money too easy.

- Pay attention to taking on monthly obligations that don't seem that big. "Small leaks sink big ships." Before adding that monthly subscription to your expenses, think about how much it will cost you annually.

- Calculate your net hourly wage. When you consider a purchase, calculate how long you would have to work to buy it. For example, if you make fifty dollars per hour gross, you probably make thirty-five dollars per hour net. If dinner and a movie cost one hundred dollars, you would have to work three hours to pay for them.

- Live each day as if it were your last but plan your finances as if you'll live forever.

- Invest in insurance to protect against catastrophic loss: health, life, disability, auto, and homeowner's or renter's insurance. To save money, get higher deductibles. Also, make sure your upper limits cover your total assets.

- Begin with term life insurance to get the most coverage for your dollar.

- Have only one credit card (unless you need one for business—then have two).

- Avoid purchasing anything with a credit card unless you have the money to pay for it when the bill comes due. Interest on credit cards is exorbitant and cannot be deducted from your taxes.

---

[15] Joe Resendiz, "Average Credit Card Debt in America: 2021," *ValuePenguin*, accessed March 2021, https://www.valuepenguin.com/average-credit-card-debt.

- Never use money to get power or control. Sometimes money is used as an unhealthy way to control a spouse.

- Avoid trendy consumerism. *The Millionaire Next Door* says most millionaires live in their homes for twenty years. Most have never spent more than $400 on a suit or $250 on a watch. Millionaires are not extravagant spenders, but neither do they deprive themselves. They are not into trendy consumerism, which is the worst kind of consumption because it costs the most money. It could be said that a rich person is not the one who has the most material goods, but the person who is content with the least.

YOU MAY NEED FINANCIAL COUNSELING

If you fall into one of the following four categories, you may need professional help:

IMPULSIVE SPENDER

If you often buy things that catch your eye that you don't need, you may be an impulsive spender.

COMPULSIVE SPENDER

If you have an uncontrollable urge to spend money when upset, you are a compulsive spender. You are responding inappropriately to an emotional need rather than responding to an actual purchasing need.

SPECIAL-INTEREST SPENDER

If the stereo in your car is more expensive than your car, you may be a special-interest spender. It's okay to spend discretionary income on a special interest you enjoy (most people do) but do it responsibly and within budget.

STATUS-SEEKING SPENDER

If you spend money you don't have on items you don't need to impress people you don't like, then you may be a status-seeking spender.

"God has given us two hands—one to receive with and the other to give with" — Billy Graham

WHAT ARE THE THREE BEST INVESTMENTS?

1. INVEST IN GOD AND HIS WORK

All money and wealth are God's. Billy Graham said, "God has given us two hands—one to receive with and the other to give with. We are not cisterns made for hoarding; we are channels made for giving."[16] You cannot outgive God.

2. INVEST IN A HOME

In the United States a primary residence is the only investment you can live in, receive tax deductions from, and sell after living in it for only two years, having the entire profit tax-exempt (up to $500,000 per couple). In addition, you can take advantage of the principle of leverage. To understand leverage, look at these two scenarios:

- You purchase a home for $500,000 cash. The home appreciates 10 percent. The return on your investment of $500,000 is $50,000, or 10 percent.

- You purchase a home for $500,000. You put $100,000 down and finance the balance. The home appreciates 10% on the total value of the home. The return on your cash investment of $100,000 would be $50,000 or a 50 percent return. So, you receive a 50 percent return instead of a 10 percent return. This is the principle of leverage.

3. INVEST IN A RETIREMENT ACCOUNT

Many couples do not make their retirement account a priority. They postpone investing, believing they can address it later when they have extra money. However, people are living longer, and the Social Security surplus funds are becoming depleted. "According to the 2021 annual report of the Social Security Board of Trustees, the surplus in the trust funds that disburse retirement, disability and other Social Security benefits will be depleted by 2034. That's one year earlier than the trustees projected in their 2020 report." That is why it is best to begin building a personal retirement account as early as possible—some believe even before buying a home. A retirement account allows pre-taxed income to be deposited into an investment without paying taxes on the initial investment or the gain until the funds are removed in retirement. The amount you defer on taxes each year gains interest. You can take money out during retirement when you are likely in a lower tax bracket.

---

[16] Billy Graham, "Billy Graham Quotes," *BrainyQuote*, accessed June 25, 2012, http://www.brainyquote.com/quotes/authors/b/billy_graham.html.

TIPS FOR INVESTING

After investing in God, a home, and a retirement account, you can discuss other investment options. Here are some tips:

STAY AWAY FROM GET-RICH-QUICK SCHEMES

They seldom work, and if one does, it will tempt you to look for another, and you'll likely lose it all. Sometimes the best investments are the ones we don't make.

INVEST IN WHAT YOU UNDERSTAND

If you don't have expertise in an area, seek a professional's opinion. Before hiring a financial advisor, do your homework. Always check references. Some financial advisors charge fees, others make commissions, and some work with a combination of the two. It may be best to hire a financial advisor who charges an hourly fee or a set fee so that they are motivated to put your investment in the best instrument, not the one that makes them the biggest commission.

NEVER BORROW MONEY TO INVEST

If your investment does not work, you are stuck with the debt to repay.

CREATE MEMORIES

If you are the head of the finances in your family and you are one of the 10 percent in society who is incredibly frugal, be sure to spend some money creating memories with your family. Taking vacations, buying gifts, and celebrating special days and achievements can help accomplish this.

If you practice sound financial principles with what you have today, then your finances will gradually grow, and you'll be able to manage whatever finances come your way.

COMPLETE THE QUESTIONS ON THE FOLLOWING PAGES

Session 6 | Chapter 16 | Finances

*Please answer all of the following questions independently of your fiancé. Do not compare your answers until our next session. However, work together **with** your fiancé to complete the budget and financial statement.*

1. On a scale of 1 to 10 (10 being best), how good is your ability to manage money?

2. Will you have joint accounts, separate accounts, or both?

3. Which one of you will pay the bills? Why?

4. Fill in the blank. I think any *discretionary* purchase over the following amount should require the agreement of both the husband and the wife:

   $ _____

5. Identify an area where your fiancé spends money for which you don't understand the value or importance.

Together Forever | God's Design for Marriage

6. If you received unexpected cash of $100,000, how do you recommend spending it as a couple?

7. What do you believe your current FICO score is? Your partner's?

8. What is your biggest concern for your future finances as a couple?

9. Complete an Annual Budget and a Financial Statement of Net Worth together with your fiancé. You can use the guides on the following pages to assist you.

ANNUAL BUDGET

- To figure out the percentage, divide the annual amount of the expense by your annual net income.
- Your total annual budget should match your annual net income.
- Your annual net income is your gross income minus all payroll deductions.
- If you have more income than expenses, add the additional amount to savings to balance your budget.

Use line 14 for anything not covered in 1 through 13.

CATEGORY	PERCENTAGE	ANNUAL AMT
1. Giving to God	%	$
2. Housing (mortgage or rent)	%	$
3. Food	%	$
4. Car payment(s)	%	$
5. Insurance (home, car, health, life, etc.)	%	$
6. Debt	%	$
7. Medical/dental	%	$
8. Clothing	%	$
9. Savings	%	$
10. Entertainment/recreation	%	$
11. Utilities	%	$
12. Cell phones	%	$
13. Cable bill	%	$
14. Other	%	$
TOTAL*	100%	$

*Must equal your annual net income.

Session 6 | Chapter 16 | Finances

FINANCIAL STATEMENT OF NET WORTH

- Complete the Financial Statement of Net Worth with your fiancé.

ASSETS	AMOUNT
1. Cash (savings, checking, money market, etc.)	$
2. Stocks, mutual funds, bonds	$
3. Partnerships	$
4. Home (current market value)	$
5. Other real estate (current market value)	$
6. Notes and Deeds of Trust (for which you are the beneficiary)	$
7. Retirement account	$
8. Furnishings (estimate cash value)	$
9. Automobile (current low Blue Book)	$
10. Collections	$
11. Miscellaneous (any other assets)	$
12. TOTAL VALUE OF ASSETS (SUM)	$
LIABILITIES	**AMOUNT**
13. Mortgage (current payoff)	$
14. Automobile loans	$
15. Credit card debt	$
16. Other loans	$
17. Outstanding bills	$
18. Misc. (any other liabilities)	$
19. TOTAL LIABILITIES (SUM)	$
TOTALS	**AMOUNT**
20. Total assets (from 12 above)	$
21. Total liabilities (from 19 above)	$
22. NET WORTH (DIFFERENCE)	$

SESSION SIX

Chapter 17

MARRIAGE GOALS

*Commit to the LORD whatever you do,
and your plans will succeed — Proverbs 16:3*

ONE OF OUR FAVORITE FAMILY VACATION SPOTS IS THE LAKE. WE especially enjoy watching sailboats serenely gliding along the water. When a boat sails from one port to another, it doesn't sail in a straight line. As the winds shift, the captain constantly tacks back and forth, correcting his direction to stay on course.

Marriage requires the same type of navigation. To think that you will always be on course is unrealistic. That is why it is important to steer your marriage intentionally and thoughtfully in the direction God wants it to go.

By participating in this premarital mentoring program, you've chosen to enter your marriage with the proper intentionality. We want to finish by helping you put into place a strategy that will help you nurture and grow your marriage in the oneness with which God wants to bless you. "In his heart a man plans his course, but the LORD determines his steps" (Proverbs 16:9).

An essential step towards navigating well in marriage is setting goals that please God. So, let's look at some basic steps for setting successful goals and establishing future plans for your marriage that will please the Lord.

SETTING YOUR GOALS

1. BRAINSTORM THE GOALS YOU WANT TO SET

When setting goals for your marriage, come together as a couple. Both of you should have a say in the plans. If only one of you makes the goals, it will be like one hand clapping. You want to operate as a team. Be willing to compromise in order to find agreement on the goals you set. After discussing all possible goals, decide on a few positive goals that you both can be excited about achieving.

2. PRAY FOR GOD'S GUIDANCE IN YOUR GOALS

Proverbs 3:5–6 says, "Trust in the LORD with all your heart and lean not on your own understanding; in all your ways acknowledge Him, and He will make your paths straight." How foolish that we try to journey through life in our own will when God promises, "'For I know the plans I have for you,' declares the LORD, 'plans to prosper you and not to harm you, plans to give you hope and a future'" (Jeremiah 29:11). We may not know what our future holds, but we know who holds our future: GOD! And He has great plans for us! Consult with Him first.

3. WRITE DOWN YOUR GOALS

Be specific when writing down your goals and set a timeline for accomplishing them. Research shows that those who write down their goals achieve significantly more than those who do not.[17] Writing down goals clarifies thinking and makes our goals more tangible.

4. CREATE ACTION STEPS FOR EACH GOAL AND SET A SPECIFIC TIME TO PUT YOUR PLAN INTO ACTION

Simply writing down a goal and believing you will achieve it is usually not enough. Action steps along the way will help you make progress on your goals. For example, if your goal is to join a small group, you might make the following action steps: (1) Contact the church to find out what small groups are available; (2) set a time and place for you and your spouse to discuss the best small group for you; and (3) set a date when you will call the small group leader to express your interest in joining the group. Remember, the way we live our days is how we live our lives. If we live our days without intentionally taking action, our lives will reflect the inaction, and we will not progress towards our goals.

An important step towards navigating well in marriage is setting goals that please God.

5. REVIEW YOUR GOALS

Set a time to periodically review your goals to ensure that you are on track. At that point, you can either celebrate achieving your designated action steps or make the needed adjustments.

CATEGORIES FOR ESTABLISHING GOALS

There are so many goals you and your fiancé may want to set for your marriage. To help you get started, below are a few categories you may want to consider.

SPIRITUAL GOALS

The foundational spiritual goal should always be to keep Christ at the center of your marriage. It may be manifested by joining a small group at church, committing to attend church each

---

[17] Sid Savara, "Writing Down Your Goals—The Harvard Written Goal Study. Fact or Fiction?" *Personal Development Training with Sid Savara*, accessed July 4, 2012, http://sidsavara.com/personal-productivity/fact-or fiction-the-truth-about-the-harvard-written-goal-study.

week, selecting a ministry, setting a regular time to pray as a couple, reading the Bible, etc. If you want to see God's Word become more authentic in your life, think of a personal trait you want to improve. Find a verse in the Bible that reflects the change you wish to make in this area. For example, if you often dominate conversations, you might select James 1:19: "Everyone should be quick to listen, slow to speak and slow to become angry." Focus on the verse you choose for a year and watch how God works in your life. Just imagine: after ten years of doing this, you will have improved ten of your weakest traits.

COMMIT TIME TO EACH OTHER

Make a goal to spend some special time regularly with your spouse. For example, commit to walking together three times a week, establishing a weekly date night, or taking a class together at a community college. Before all the busyness of the world closes in on you, schedule special time together.

FAMILY GOALS

Although this program focuses on your relationship as a couple, if you have additional family members close by or in your household, set some extended family goals, too. For instance, you may want to have a family game night or movie night. Or set date nights with individual family members. Perhaps you can challenge other family members to choose a Bible verse to memorize and live by for the year.

Writing down goals clarifies thinking and makes our goals more tangible.

VACATION PLANS

Sometimes financial strains on your budget limit the vacation fund, but this should not eliminate spending some fun vacation time at least once a year. The point is not how much money you spend on your vacation, but rather that you take some time off together. You can do something as simple as spending a week at home having an itinerary each day of doing something fun together. There are many things you can do together that cost little or nothing: spend a day at the beach, go on a picnic, go hiking, camp in your backyard, etc. Use your imagination and be original. Create memories!

GOALS FOR YOURSELF

Have a personal goal for yourself. Your marriage vow of becoming one does not mean you cannot have individual goals. You may want to take a dance class, join a softball league, take up a hobby, start a book club, or learn a new skill. By growing in new ways, you will remain fresh and interesting to your spouse. Encourage your spouse to set personal goals, too.

FINANCIAL GOALS

We covered financial goals in detail in the last chapter. Be sure to review these goals every year or whenever your finances change significantly. Remember, https://wwws.mint.com is a free resource that can assist you with setting and evaluating your financial objectives.

HEALTH AND FITNESS GOALS

You will enjoy each other and life more if you are healthy and fit. Set goals to help maintain your health. Be supportive of one another in this area, not critical.

You might notice we didn't list professional goals. Professional goals are important too, but make sure they leave room for giving the proper attention to your marriage. Research has shown that when marriage is kept in its rightful place in your priorities, it will benefit you in every other layer of your life.[18] There is nothing more critical to your career success than having a joyful marriage.

COMPLETE THE QUESTIONS ON THE FOLLOWING PAGES

---

[18] Tyler Ward, "3 Things I Wish I Knew Before We God Married," *Tyler Ward Is*, accessed December 8, 2014, http://www.tylerwardis.com/3-things-i-wish-i-knew-before-we-got-married/#more-794.

Session 6 | Chapter 17 | Marriage Goals

Please answer the following questions independently of your fiancé.
Do not compare your answers until our next session.

1. What Bible verse would you like to commit to memory this year? This verse should focus on helping you improve one area in your life.

2. List some of your ideas for goals in the following areas:

TYPE OF GOAL / GOAL IDEAS
Spiritual
Time with each other
Family

Session 6 | Chapter 17 | Marriage Goals

TYPE OF GOAL / GOAL IDEAS
Vacation
Personal
Health and fitness

3. Make a date with your fiancé to develop goals as a couple for the year. Write the specific date, time, and place below.

SESSION SIX

Chapter 18

KEEPING THE FLAME GOING

*The fear of the LORD is the beginning of wisdom,
and knowledge of the Holy One is understanding — Proverbs 9:10*

THE PURPOSE OF THIS PREMARITAL MENTORING PROGRAM IS TO REVEAL God's blueprint for marriage. The intent was not to build the house for you but to give you the tools and the materials to build your own home following God's blueprint.

We were recently in a coffee shop and overheard an older man at a nearby table say to his wife with a chuckle, "If I had known I was going to live this long, I would have taken better care of myself." Looking back on your life with regrets is no fun. Hindsight gives clarity and insight. There are many ways we could complete the man's statement, "If I had known _____, I would have _____." We have presented you with considerable information throughout these six sessions. Now it is up to you to put the concepts presented into practice so you don't have regrets.

Knowledge fades with time unless you refresh what you have learned. This chapter is designed to provide a resource so that you can periodically review what you have learned and give your marriage a tune-up.

Here is how it works. After you are married, set a time at least quarterly to review the twenty-one questions below with your spouse. Hopefully, you will answer most of the questions with a positive response. However, some of your responses will likely reveal that your relationship needs some improvement in those areas. Each question will be followed with some encouragement on that topic and will direct you to the chapter in your workbook where you can refresh that area of your relationship.

Read all twenty-one questions before answering the three homework questions at the end of this chapter.

TWENTY-ONE QUESTIONS

1. ARE ALL THREE TYPES OF LOVE (EROS, PHILIA, AND AGAPE) PRESENT IN YOUR MARRIAGE?

Review the list you wrote of ten things you love about your fiancé in Chapter 2. Discuss together how you can each express the three types of love towards each other more fully. Keep this list available and refer to it often. Whenever you become discouraged about your marriage, reread the list of things you love about your partner. One of the most effective tools for overcoming marital disappointment is replacing a negative thought about your husband or wife with thoughts of gratitude. Studies show that we can focus on only one emotion at a time: choose love. (Refer to Chapter 2.)

2. HAVE YOU BOTH FORGIVEN EACH OTHER FOR EVERYTHING?

Make sure forgiveness flows freely between you and your spouse for BIG and small conflicts. Practice forgiving, not collecting, hurts. God has forgiven us for all our sins. He wants us to forgive one another freely. "Bear with each other and forgive whatever grievances you may have against one another. Forgive as the Lord forgave you" (Colossians 3:13). We forgive by faith, out of obedience to God. God wants us to love others and to love Him. This love He speaks of is a choice, not a feeling. We must trust God to complete His work in us. Make it between you and God and not between you and your spouse. Turn your heart over to God. Corrie ten Boom, a Christian who survived a Nazi concentration camp, said, "Forgiveness is the key that unlocks the door of resentment and the handcuffs of hatred. It is a power that breaks the chains of bitterness and the shackles of selfishness."[19] One of the most loving actions you can continually take is forgiving. (Refer to Chapter 3.)

3. ARE YOU LIVING OUT THE BIBLICAL ROLES OUTLINED FOR A HUSBAND AND WIFE IN EPHESIANS 5:21–33?

We each need to worshipfully surrender our lives to Christ. Ultimately, a wife answers to God for how well she submits to her husband's leadership, whether or not he is making good, loving decisions. Ultimately, a husband answers to God for how well he loves his wife, regardless of whether or not she respects and submits to him.

When your spouse falls short of living out God's will in your marriage, take your frustrations to God. Trust God to meet your needs, and He will fill you with His love to take back to the marriage. In doing this, instead of expecting perfect behavior from two imperfect people, you'll look for the perfect response from your perfect God. (Refer to Chapter 4.)

---

[19] Corrie ten Boom, *Clippings from My Notebook* (Nashville: Thomas Nelson, 1982), pg 19.

4. ARE YOU CONTINUING TO PRAY TOGETHER OFTEN?

If not, start by setting a time at least once a week to pray together. Remember, God wants to bless your marriage beyond your imagination, but you need to invite Him in and follow His will together. There is nothing more important than keeping God at the center of your marriage. (Refer to Chapter 4.)

5. DO YOU CONTINUE TO SHARE HOW, SPECIFICALLY, YOUR SPOUSE CAN PRAY FOR YOU?

Prayer is one of the most loving, intimate expressions that can be exchanged between a husband and wife. After you share your prayer requests, pray out loud together for each other. (Refer to Chapter 4.)

6. IS YOUR SPOUSE MEETING YOUR MOST IMPORTANT WANTS AND NEEDS?

You may desire a weekly date night; time to talk about light topics; fun together doing a hobby; more frequent sex; more transparency with the finances; more home cooking; being more physically active; entertaining more (or less) with family and friends; hearing more affirming statements; having more intimate, open, honest conversations; etc. Lovingly share your desires with your spouse.

We should not look to our spouse to make us happy. There will be times in your marriage when it will be more profitable to take the focus off your partner meeting your wants and put your focus on God. Philippians 4:19 assures us, "God will meet all your needs according to His glorious riches in Christ Jesus." Bob and Judy Hughes' book, *Love Focused*, is an excellent resource to understand this concept better. They also have a couples Bible study you could do together. (Refer to Chapter 5.)

7. HAVE YOU ESTABLISHED A WEEKLY KING FOR THE DAY AND QUEEN FOR THE DAY?

Share with each other what you would like for your spouse to do for you on your day. Be attentive to meeting your spouse's wishes on their day. Remember, this can be a real game changer. (Refer to Chapter 5.)

8. ARE THERE ANY AREAS IN WHICH YOU FEEL YOUR SPOUSE IS NOT SUCCESSFULLY FULFILLING THEIR ROLE IN MARRIAGE?

God gives specific instructions for husbands to love their wives as Christ loved the church. God instructs wives to respect their husbands and submit to their leadership in the family. This does not mean that a husband controls all areas of marriage. Instead, a godly leader recognizes the best gifted in given areas and gives jurisdiction for those responsibilities to the best-qualified person. Lovingly discuss any roles you would like to see changed or improved, and share what betterment looks like to you. (Refer to Chapter 5.)

9. ARE YOU SPENDING MOST OF YOUR TIME IN THE SWEET SPOT?

A marriage has momentum in the direction of the sweet spot or the sour patch. If you are not spending most of your time in the sweet spot, go back and review the eighteen skills for staying in the sweet spot. Remember, fun is the litmus test of a good relationship. Do something fun together. (Refer to Chapter 6.)

10. ARE YOU DEALING EFFECTIVELY WITH YOUR INCOMPATIBILITIES?

A great marriage is not based on marrying someone compatible because God does not make any two people perfectly compatible; it is based on learning how to deal effectively with your incompatibilities. If you are struggling with compatibility, consider taking a Myers-Briggs Type Indicator® instrument to identify your personality styles (http://www.16personalities.com offers a free test online). Remember, there is no right or wrong to personality differences. You are both created in the image of God. Work on becoming more understanding and accepting of the fact that you approach life differently. (Refer to Chapter 7.)

11. ARE THE DIFFERENCES BETWEEN MEN AND WOMEN CAUSING FRICTION IN YOUR MARRIAGE?

Men and women have very different operating systems. We will never completely understand each other, but we can educate ourselves on what is important to each other. The book *Love and Respect* by Emerson Eggerrichs gives a deeper understanding of our differences. You may want to consider reading the book together. Ultimately, God wants our differences to complement and complete each other in marriage as we work together as one. (Refer to Chapter 8.)

12. HOW FULL IS YOUR LOVE TANK ON A SCALE OF 1 TO 10? WHAT CAN YOUR SPOUSE DO TO MAKE IT A 10?

Remember to speak to your spouse in their love language and remind your spouse to talk to you in your language. In addition, you may want to read the book, *The Five Love Languages* by Gary Chapman. (Refer to Chapter 9.)

13. ARE THERE ANY ISSUES WITH YOUR FAMILY RELATIONSHIPS CAUSING PROBLEMS IN YOUR MARRIAGE?

Discuss what you can do to improve any family tension. Be sure that your relationship with each other is kept primary and that you always show a united front. When problems arise with your family, face them together. Discuss them together as husband and wife. Pray about them together. If needed, seek outside counsel from trusted advisors or professionals. With kids, keep things in perspective. Don't major in minors. If it is not life-altering for your child, natural consequences may be the best teacher. If extended family members are causing issues, sometimes it is best to set healthy boundaries to protect your primary family relationships. (Refer to Chapter 10.)

14. ARE YOU COMMUNICATING WITH EACH OTHER EFFECTIVELY?

Content, tone, and body language are all essential aspects of communication but listening and choosing the appropriate time for sensitive conversations are also important. Work on any weaknesses in your communication. When couples have trouble with communication, it is often a symptom of a bigger issue. Try to identify the more significant problem and work that through using the tools offered through this program such as the "Ten Rules to Resolve Conflict" in Appendix 7. Above all, always speak to each other in love using the "Rules for Discussion" in Appendix 6. (Refer to Chapter 11.)

15. DO YOU HAVE ANY UNRESOLVED CONFLICTS IN YOUR MARRIAGE?

Conflicts come in all shapes and sizes. With moderate disputes, use the *Start or Stop and Continue Method*. Also, holding your spouse's hand and praying together can often soften hearts to restore peace. However, if you have a major conflict, set a time to use the "Ten Rules to Resolve Conflict" in Appendix 7 to resolve your dispute. (Refer to Chapter 12.)

16. ARE YOU ENJOYING THE EMOTIONAL INTIMACY YOU DESIRE WITH YOUR SPOUSE?

You should feel comfortable and safe sharing your most intimate thoughts and dreams with each other. It is as if you are saying, "into-me-see." Growing in this area involves continual effort and investment in your relationship. (Refer to Chapter 13.)

17. DO YOU HAVE A VIBRANT SEX LIFE?

If your love life isn't all that you would like it to be, the best way to revitalize your physical intimacy is to communicate openly and honestly with each other. Truthfully communicate your desires to your spouse. Be sensitive and loving in fulfilling your partner's wishes. Try something fun like showering together. (Refer to Chapter 14.)

18. IS YOUR MARRIAGE SAFELY AFFAIR-PROOFED?

It's too late to prevent an affair after it's happened. Protect your marriage by keeping proper boundaries in place. It is imperative that you give each other full access to all your communication devices and social networking sites. Discuss if there are any areas that need to be reinforced. (Refer to Chapter 15.)

19. ARE YOUR FINANCES HEALTHY?

Be transparent with each other with your spending. Recognize that you will likely have different ways you will each want to spend discretionary income. Provided it fits into your budget, be understanding of your differences. A budget and financial statement are good ways to keep track of your finances. A helpful tool for creating a budget and maintaining transparency with your finances is https://www.mint.com. If you need some extra guidance on your finances, many churches offer financial counseling following either Dave Ramsey's principles or Crown Ministries. Find information on these programs at www.daveramsey.com and www.crown.org. (Refer to Chapter 16.)

Session 6 | Chapter 18 | Keeping the Flame Going

20. HAVE YOU SET GOALS TOGETHER AS A COUPLE?

One of the cornerstones of this program is having an intentional marriage. Relationships are either getting better or getting worse. They don't stay the same. Therefore, it is important to continue pursuing goals and dreams as a couple. For this to happen, you need to set goals and take action steps. In order for goals to truly take hold, they should be written down and reviewed for progress. (Refer to Chapter 17.)

21. ARE YOU INVOLVED IN A SMALL GROUP FOR COUPLES?

Fellowship with other believers is one of the conduits God uses to share His truth with us. Communing with other Christian married couples will help enrich your marriage through shared life experiences and godly insights. (Refer to Chapter 17.)

In most cases, these steps will be enough to put your marriage back on track. However, in some instances, you may need additional help. If you feel that your relationship may need additional help, talk with your pastor or a professional counselor for guidance. Your marriage is important. Take the proper steps to ensure that you experience God's best.

Have you ever noticed that the Bible begins and ends with a marriage? It begins with the coming together of Adam and Eve: "For this reason a man will leave his father and mother and be united to his wife, and they will become one flesh" (Genesis 2:24). It ends with believers being joined with Christ in marriage at the wedding supper of the Lamb (Revelation 19). The marriage relationship is a picture of the relationship God desires to have with each of us. God did not intend to have a distant relationship with people. He created us to have a loving relationship with Him now and for eternity. By keeping a focus on Christ in your relationship during good times and the struggles, you will live out God's design for marriage and build a marriage that lasts a lifetime!

COMPLETE THE QUESTIONS ON THE FOLLOWING PAGES

Session 6 | Chapter 18 | Keeping the Flame Going

Please answer the following question independently of your fiancé.
Do not compare your answers until our next session.

1. In taking inventory on your relationship today using the questions above, which areas did you identify as still needing growth? Be honest. Please list the numbers of those questions.

2. Decide the dates for your quarterly marriage assessment and tune-up. Write the dates below.

3. Turn back to read page 15 and read your answer to question 2 (Chapter 1). How well did you achieve what you were hoping to accomplish through this program?

NOTES

WHAT IT MEANS TO BE A GODLY HUSBAND

THE BIBLE SAYS THE SPIRIT, WHO IS IN EVERY BELIEVER, PRODUCES ACTS of godliness, "love, joy, peace, patience, kindness, goodness, faithfulness, gentleness, self-control" (Galatians 5:22–23). Godliness involves a genuine striving to imitate Christ, to be like Him in thought and action. These characteristics of a godly disposition apply to every believer, whether male or female. Husbands are given additional instructions on how to be Christlike husbands.

"Husbands, love your wives, just as Christ loved the church and gave himself up for her…In this same way, husbands ought to love their wives as their own bodies. He who loves his wife loves himself. After all, no one ever hated his own body, but he feeds and cares for it, just as Christ does the church—for we are members of His body." (Ephesians 5:25 & 28-30). In this passage, husbands are being called into a very deep, sacrificial, unconditional love. Christ loved the church so much that, even while we were still sinners, He went to the cross and died for us.

Philippians 2:3-4 says, "Do nothing out of selfish ambition or vain conceit. Rather, in humility, value others above yourselves, not looking to your own interests but each of you to the interests of the others." In marriage, this can be particularly difficult. It may mean you need to forgo watching that big game to attend a family function. It is not easy doing what is most loving when it is different from what you want. We need to remember to consider the feelings and ideas of our wives, rather than assuming they think as we do.

Husbands are also given the role of leadership in the marriage. Godly leadership is not a dictatorship. This does not mean that a husband controls all areas of marriage. Instead, a godly leader recognizes who has the best giftedness in given areas and gives jurisdiction for those responsibilities to the best-qualified person.

SPIRITUAL LEADERSHIP

God holds men responsible for the spiritual and physical well-being of their families. Therefore, an ongoing personal relationship with Jesus is crucial when leading a family spiritually. Here are some specific ways you can be an effective spiritual leader of the family.

PRAY FOR YOUR WIFE AND FAMILY
Have a disciplined set time that you pray daily. Also, pray randomly, especially when special needs arise.

PRAY TOGETHER WITH YOUR WIFE
Have a disciplined set time that you pray together with your wife. Many couples pray in bed together every day. Praying with and for your wife at the end of the day can be some of the best foreplay. If you have children, praying together as a family at least once a week will bond you

in a special way. When our kids were still at home, we used to meet twenty minutes before we would normally leave for church each week to pray as a family. If you regularly pray together, it will be natural to pray together when special needs arise.

ATTEND CHURCH REGULARLY

Many Christians will attend church when it is convenient. Make attending church as a family a priority.

SPEND TIME IN GOD'S WORD

Regular Bible reading is an important way to help us understand how better to surrender our lives to the Lordship of Jesus Christ. This is also how God can talk to us. A more thorough understanding of the Bible gives us a more Christlike worldview.

JOIN A COUPLE'S SMALL GROUP

A meaningful way to grow in our Christian walk is to fellowship with other believers. Joining a small group will allow you to do life with others who share your values.

GIVE YOUR TIME, TALENTS, AND TREASURES TO GOD

A great way to give your time and talents is to get involved in a ministry. For example, when Angie and I got involved in the premarital mentoring program at church, we did it to give back to God. Little did we know that God was going to pour out blessings on us. In Malachi 3:10, God asks us to test Him. "'Bring the whole tithe into the storehouse, that there may be food in my house. Test me in this,' 'says the Lord Almighty,' 'and see if I will not throw open the floodgates of heaven and pour out so much blessing that there will not be room enough to store it.'" That is a great promise.

MAKE GODLY DECISIONS

Big decisions require God at the center. When you have a decision to make, pray about it, see what the Bible has to say about it, listen carefully to what your wife has to say about it, seek the counsel of Christian mentors, and then make your decision.

BE TENDER TOWARDS YOUR WIFE

The Bible also says, "Husbands, love your wives and do not be harsh with them" (Colossians 3:19). Men have deeper, stronger voices that can sound harsh and intimidating to their wives. It is valuable to understand this and use a loving tone with your wife.

First Peter 3:7 says, "Husbands, in the same way be considerate as you live with your wives, and treat them with respect as the weaker partner and as heirs with you of the gracious gift of life, so that nothing will hinder your prayers." Within the context of this verse, "weaker" does not mean that the wife is in any way "less than" her husband; it means that a woman is not to be treated as "one of the guys." A wise husband will be understanding of this and be sensitive to the differences. A wife desires to be treasured and cherished by her husband.

As you enter marriage, your first ministry is to love and lead your wife. When a husband is consistent in the spiritual leadership of his marriage, it is natural for his wife to respect and follow his lead.

WHAT IT MEANS TO BE A SUBMISSIVE WIFE

THE BIBLE SAYS THE SPIRIT, WHO IS IN EVERY BELIEVER, PRODUCES ACTS of godliness, "love, joy, peace, patience, kindness, goodness, faithfulness, gentleness, self-control" (Galatians 5:22–23). Godliness involves a genuine striving to imitate Christ, to be like Him in thought and action. These characteristics of a godly disposition apply to every believer, whether male or female. The Bible gives even more specific qualifications about what a godly wife looks like.

Proverbs 31 gives a beautiful word picture of a godly wife. Her husband has complete trust in her. The passage describes her as being devoted, dignified, wise, hard-working, and industrious. She takes care of her household. She takes care of herself. She cares for the poor. But, most of all, she loves the Lord and maintains an attitude of joy.

Ephesians 5:21-24 further tells how wives are to conduct themselves, "Submit to one another out of reverence for Christ. Wives, submit yourselves to your own husbands as you do to the Lord. For the husband is the head of the wife as Christ is the head of the church, His body, of which He is the Savior. Now as the church submits to Christ, so also wives should submit to their husbands in everything."

Ultimately, when a wife submits to her husband, she does it out of obedience to God. Jesus (who is co-equal and co-eternal with God the Father and the Holy Spirit) modeled submission to us by perfectly doing the will of God the Father in everything He said and did on earth. A wife should follow this example by worshipfully surrendering her life to Christ by:

- Following her husband's leadership
- Respecting and trusting her husband's opinion
- Seeking her husband's counsel when making decisions
- Believing in her husband's ability to succeed in his areas of responsibility
- Being her husband's helpmate
- Honoring her husband by talking about him in a positive way
- Praising, affirming, and appreciating her husband
- Being a team player
- Being her husband's No. 1 fan!
- Serving her husband with sacrificial love

Appendix 2 | What it Means to be a Submissive Wife

- Avoiding nonbiblical criticism or nagging
- Not comparing him unfavorably to others
- Be sensitive that your words are not blaming or controlling him
- Avoid correcting him in front of others

For a wife to be submissive to her husband as Christ was submissive to the Father means she willingly allows her husband to lead. A wife will ultimately answer to God for how well she submits to her husband's leadership whether he is making good, loving decisions or not. Likewise, her husband will answer to God for how well he leads and loves her. However, a wife should not follow her husband into sinful behavior, for God is her ultimate authority.

When a wife is not happy with the direction her husband is leading, she should take her frustrations to God with an open teachable spirit. God may be doing work inside of her through her obedience to submit. God may be protecting her through her husband's direction over what she feels is best. God may want her to lovingly share her thoughts with her husband on why they should follow a different path. God may want to work on her husband's heart while she submits her desires to the Lord. God does not need her to be the Holy Spirit or a "holy nag." God wants her to trust him to meet her needs and give her the proper response.

God ultimately wants you to operate together as one with your husband. Therefore, pray for God to either change your husband's mind or change your heart. In doing this, instead of requiring perfect behavior from two imperfect people, you are looking for the ideal protection and guidance from our perfect God.

As you grow more intimate in your relationship with Christ, you will grow increasingly godly in your marriage.

THE FIVE LOVE LANGUAGES TEST FOR WOMEN

Circle the letter that corresponds to the answer that most accurately describes how you feel. Circle only one letter in each numbered set of questions.[20]

1. Sweet notes from my partner make me feel good. — A

   I love my partner's hugs. — E

2. I like to be alone with my partner. — B

   I feel loved when my partner washes my car. — D

3. Receiving special gifts from my partner makes me happy. — C

   I enjoy long trips with my partner. — B

4. I feel loved when my partner helps me wash the car. — D

   I like it when my partner touches me. — E

5. I feel loved when my partner puts his arm around me. — E

   I know my partner loves me because he surprises me with gifts. — C

6. I like going most anywhere with my partner. — B

   I like to hold my partner's hand. — E

7. I value the gifts my partner gives me. — C

   I love to hear my partner say he loves me. — A

8. I like my partner to sit close to me. — E

   My partner tells me I look good, and I like that. — A

---

[20] Gary Chapman, "Love Languages Personal Profiles: For Wives," *5 Love Languages*®, accessed June 27, 2021, http://www.5lovelanguages.com/assessments/love/.

Appendix 3 | The Five Love Languages Test for Women

9.	Spending time with my partner makes me happy.	B
	Even the smallest gift from my partner is important to me.	C
10.	I feel loved when my partner tells me he is proud of me.	A
	When my partner helps clean up, I know he loves me.	D
11.	No matter what we do, I love doing things with my partner.	B
	Supportive comments from my partner make me feel good.	A
12.	Little things my partner does for me mean more to me than things he says.	D
	I love to hug my partner.	E
13.	My partner's praise means a lot to me.	A
	It means a lot to me that my partner gives me gifts I really like.	C
14.	Just being around my partner makes me feel good.	B
	I love it when my partner gives me a massage.	E
15.	My partner's reactions to my accomplishments are so encouraging.	A
	It means a lot to me when my partner helps with something I know he hates.	D
16.	I never get tired of my partner's kisses.	E
	I love that my partner shows genuine interest in the things I like to do.	B
17.	I can count on my partner to help me with projects.	D
	I still get excited when opening a gift from my partner.	C
18.	I love for my partner to compliment my appearance.	A
	I love that my partner listens to me and respects my ideas.	B
19.	I can't help but touch my partner when he's close by.	E
	My partner sometimes runs errands for me, and I appreciate that.	D

Appendix 3 | The Five Love Languages Test for Women

20. My partner deserves an award for all the things he does to help me. — D

I'm sometimes amazed at how thoughtful my partner's gifts to me are. — C

21. I love having my partner's undivided attention. — B

I love that my partner helps clean the house. — D

22. I look forward to seeing what my partner gives me for my birthday. — C

I never get tired of hearing my partner tell me that I am important to him. — A

23. My partner lets me know he loves me by giving me gifts. — C

My partner shows his love by helping me without me having to ask. — D

24. My partner doesn't interrupt me when I am talking, and I like that. — B

I never get tired of receiving gifts from my partner. — C

25. My partner is good about asking how he can help when I'm tired. — D

It doesn't matter where we go; I just like going places with my partner. — B

26. I love cuddling with my partner. — E

I love surprise gifts from my partner. — C

27. My partner's encouraging words give me confidence. — A

I love to watch movies with my partner. — B

28. I couldn't ask for any better gifts than the ones my partner gives me. — C

I love it that my partner can't keep his hands off me. — E

29. It means a lot to me when my partner helps me despite being busy. — D

It makes me feel really good when my partner tells me he appreciates me. — A

30. I love hugging and kissing my partner after we've been apart for a while. — E

I love hearing my partner tell me that he believes in me. — A

Together Forever | God's Design for Marriage

Appendix 4

THE FIVE LOVE LANGUAGES TEST FOR MEN

Circle the letter that corresponds to the answer that most accurately describes how you feel. Circle only one letter in each numbered set of questions.[21]

1.	My partner's love notes make me feel good.	A
	I love my partner's hugs.	E
2.	I like to be alone with my partner.	B
	I feel loved when my partner helps me do yard work.	D
3.	Receiving special gifts from my partner makes me happy.	C
	I enjoy long trips with my partner.	B
4.	I feel loved when my partner does my laundry.	D
	I like it when my partner touches me.	E
5.	I feel loved when my partner puts her arm around me.	E
	I know my partner loves me because she surprises me with gifts.	C
6.	I like going most anywhere with my partner.	B
	I like to hold my partner's hand.	E
7.	I value the gifts my partner gives me.	C
	I love to hear my partner say she loves me.	A
8.	I like my partner to sit close to me.	E
	My partner tells me I look good, and I like that.	A

---

[20] Gary Chapman, "Love Languages Personal Profiles: For Wives," *5 Love Languages*®, accessed June 27, 2021, http://www.5lovelanguages.com/assessments/love/.

9. Spending time with my partner makes me happy. — B

Even the smallest gift from my partner is important to me. — C

10. I feel loved when my partner tells me she is proud of me. — A

When my partner cooks a meal for me, I know she loves me. — D

11. No matter what we do, I love doing things with my partner. — B

Supportive comments from my partner make me feel good. — A

12. Little things my partner does for me mean more to me than things she says. — D

I love to hug my partner. — E

13. My partner's praise means a lot to me. — A

It means a lot to me that my partner gives me gifts I really like. — C

14. Just being around my partner makes me feel good. — B

I love it when my partner gives me a back rub. — E

15. My partner's reactions to my accomplishments are so encouraging. — A

It means a lot to me when my partner helps with something I know she hates. — D

16. I never get tired of my partner's kisses. — E

I love that my partner shows genuine interest in the things I like to do. — B

17. I can count on my partner to help me with projects. — D

I still get excited when opening a gift from my partner. — C

18. I love for my partner to compliment my appearance. — A

I love that my partner listens to me and respects my ideas. — B

19. I can't help but touch my partner when she's close by. — E

My partner sometimes runs errands for me, and I appreciate that. — D

Appendix 4 | The Five Love Languages Test for Men

20. My partner deserves an award for all the things she does to help me.	D
I'm sometimes amazed at how thoughtful my partner's gifts to me are.	C
21. I love having my partner's undivided attention.	B
I love that my partner helps clean the house.	D
22. I look forward to seeing what my partner gives me for my birthday.	C
I never get tired of hearing my partner tell me that I am important to her.	A
23. My partner lets me know she loves me by giving me gifts.	C
My partner shows her love by helping me catch up on projects around the house.	D
24. My partner doesn't interrupt me when I am talking, and I like that.	B
I never get tired of receiving gifts from my partner.	C
25. My partner can tell when I'm tired, and she's good about asking how she can help.	D
It doesn't matter where we go; I just like going places with my partner.	B
26. Kissing me unexpectedly excites me.	E
I love surprise gifts from my partner.	C
27. My partner's encouraging words give me confidence.	A
I love to watch movies with my partner.	B
28. I couldn't ask for any better gifts than the ones my partner gives me.	C
I love it that my partner can't keep her hands off me.	E
29. It means a lot to me when my partner helps me despite having other things to do.	D
It makes me feel really good when my partner tells me she appreciates me.	A
30. I love hugging and kissing my partner after we've been apart for a while.	E
I love hearing my partner tell me that she believes in me.	A

Appendix 5

LOVE LANGUAGES GUIDE

LOVE LANGUAGE	ACTIONS	AVOID
WORDS OF AFFIRMATION	• Compliments • Notes and cards • Kind words	• Criticism
QUALITY TIME	• One-to-one time • Face-to-face interaction • Taking long walks together • Doing activities together	• Allowing other people or priorities to interrupt our special time together
RECEIVING GIFTS	• Giving gifts on special and not-so-special days • More about the thoughtfulness of the gift than the expense of the gift	• Ignoring or forgetting special days
ACTS OF SERVICE	• Helping with chores • Saying things like, "How can I help you?"	• Helping others and not being there for your spouse
PHYSICAL TOUCH	• Touches • Hugs & cuddling • Kisses	• Negative touch

*Chart based on Gary Chapman's book, *The 5 Love Languages*®.

RULES FOR DISCUSSION

1. Speak in a quiet voice.
2. Do not interrupt.
3. Do not bring up the past.
4. Do not blame.
5. Do not use profanity.
6. Do not criticize.
7. Use "I feel" statements, not attacking "you" statements.
8. State your feelings, not your partner's.
9. Never threaten your relationship.

TEN RULES TO RESOLVE CONFLICT

1. Define the issue to be resolved.
2. Set a time to meet.
3. Set a private place to meet.
4. Begin in prayer.
5. Each share your position.
6. Each point out what you have done to contribute to the problem.
7. Each point out what you can do to help resolve the issue.
8. Agree on a resolution acceptable to both.
9. Write down the resolution.
10. End in prayer.

Appendix 8

TEN WAYS TO BE A FANTASTIC WIFE

1. Believe in your husband and be his No. 1 fan.

2. Be careful not to nag your husband. Instead, turn over your concerns to God in prayer. Ask God to give you oneness in your marriage.

3. It is not uncommon for a husband to have a greater sex drive than his wife. Take care of his sexual needs.

4. On the first day of each month, put the following question on your calendar: "What must it be like to be married to me?"

5. People tend to be what you say they are. Tell your husband what a great husband, friend, and lover he is. He won't disappoint you.

6. When you come together at the end of the day, greet him in a loving way.

7. Guys are visual; do your best to take care of yourself and be attractive to him.

8. Remember to speak in his love language.

9. Share in his hobbies with him. Continue to be the fun person he married.

10. Put Christ at the center of your life and the center of your marriage.

TEN WAYS TO BE A FANTASTIC HUSBAND

1. Always show your wife how special she is to you.

2. Avoid being too critical. What you may think of as constructive criticism, she may see as an attack on her.

3. If you want to have a great sex life, you must keep some romance in your relationship. Continue to date your wife.

4. On the first day of each month, put the following question on your calendar: "What must it be like to be married to me?"

5. Pray with your wife often. It means more to her than you know.

6. Compliment your wife's appearance. She knows you are visual. So, your compliments are important to her and make her feel special.

7. People tend to be what you say they are. Tell your wife what a great wife, friend, and lover she is. She won't disappoint you.

8. Remember to talk in her love language.

9. Your wife will need to talk. Take time to be a good listener. Often, she won't want a solution; she will just want to talk to you. Value her opinion.

10. Put Christ at the center of your life, your marriage, and be the spiritual leader of your family. Ask your wife how you can be praying for her.

www.ingramcontent.com/pod-product-compliance
Lightning Source LLC
Chambersburg PA
CBHW060424010526
44118CB00017B/2348